DECISION HEIGHT

by Jon Hilton

Copyright © 2014 by Jon Hilton

All rights reserved. No part of this publication may be reproduced, distributed, or transmitted in any form or by any means, including photocopying, recording, or other electronic or mechanical methods, without the prior written permission of the author, except in the case of brief quotations embodied in critical reviews and certain other non-commercial uses permitted by copyright law.

Seventy percent of the proceeds of any future online sales will be donated to charity (www.justgiving.com/jon-hilton). Permission was given by individuals for their pictures to be used in any future publication. Such permission was verbally agreed at the point the picture was taken. On some devices images can be enlarged by "double tapping" them.

Some of the language used, henceforth, is what could be described as "colourful". Turn the pages at your own discretion, dear reader.

And finally the rules of the air are there for the preservation of life. Anyone who subsequently decides to replicate this flight in a Microlight / Ultralight needs his mental health assessing (I'd suggest).

Jon

Published by WriterMotive
www.writermotive.co.uk

Contents

Chapter 1 – Me 1

Chapter 2 - The Aircraft 3

Chapter 3 - The Trip 6

Chapter 4 - Basic Terminology 10

Chapter 5 - Britain, Faroes, Iceland 24th May 14

Chapter 6 - Iceland, Greenland 25th May 43

Chapter 7 - Greenland 26th May 67

Chapter 8 - Greenland 27th May 72

Chapter 9 - Greenland 28th May 79

Chapter 10 - Greenland 29th May 85

Chapter 11 - Greenland 30th May 92

Chapter 12 - Greenland, Canada 31st May 101

Chapter 13 - Canada, Greenland 1st June 124

Chapter 14 - Greenland 2nd June 139

Chapter 15 - Greenland 3rd June................................. 141

Chapter 16 - Greenland 4th June 148

Chapter 17 - Greenland 5th June 162

Chapter 18 - Greenland 6th June 169

Chapter 19 - Greenland 7th June 174

Chapter 20 - Greenland, Iceland 8th June 180

Chapter 21 - Iceland, Faroes, Scotland 9th June 205

Chapter 22 - UK 10th June.. 227

Chapter 23 - Postscript - Back to reality 236

Chapter 24 - Jon Hilton, so far. 239

Chapter 25 - One Year on …….................................…245

Chapter 1 – Me

I get itchy feet, I guess. Always have done. There's something in me that makes me push myself.

I couldn't say whether it's due to my upbringing, or a fault in my DNA somewhere, but there's a continuous hunger in me to do 'things'.

Having said that the reader should be aware I'm scared of everything. Flying, crashing, physical pain, the cold, letting people down, the unknown. The list is a very long one.

I'll summarise my adventures through life at the end of the current saga. I guess you could say I've had an interesting time and I'd suggest you only think of reading it if you're very, very bored.

At present I run a small firm that deals with the legal profession. It does ok for itself. I'm not rich and I'm not poor. I have an overdraft like most folk.

Courtesy of the business I'm able to take time off when I need to and I'm quite lucky in a lot of ways.

I'm the eldest son of a Social Worker and an Insolvency Accountant. Which means I care about people's feelings but, on the downside, I can be a tight bugger.

Jon Hilton

Going off at a tangent, I also have a lot of OCD moments where I'm always bloody checking things. Drives me absolutely nuts.

Physically I'm roundabout 6ft and 13 stone. I guess I was a reasonably good looking kid but I'm not such a looker these days. 45 years have taken their toll in various ways.

From a personal perspective the last 10 years of my life have been subject to the pull of two specific, feisty, females....

If you Google Billy Connolly's, 'Wildebeest sketch' that about sums up my situation. I'm one of the Wildebeests. You'll have to go online if you're the curious type.

In short, I see myself as a cross between David Niven and Harold Lloyd with a tiny bit of Terry Thomas thrown in...

If the reader hasn't heard of any of these chaps think, 'well intentioned, a bit gungho and occasionally a tad mischievous.'

To bring things back to flying I am not the complete pilot by any means. I nearly died trying to do something no one's done before. I made mistakes and pretty much battled to stay alive each time I flew.

Anyway, all this is simply background noise.

Chapter 2 - The Aircraft

There are two types of Microlights in the UK. Namely 'Flexwings' and '3 Axis' aircraft.

The Flexwing is probably everyone's perception of the traditional Microlight. A sail above an open canopy with an engine mounted at the back. Then there's the 3 Axis Microlight which is a fixed wing aircraft.

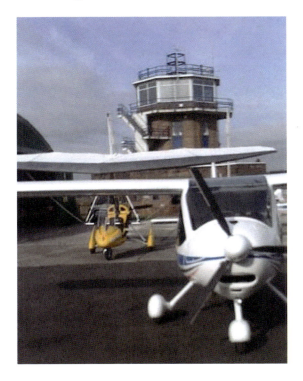

Jon Hilton

Both types began life as slightly rickety looking things that managed to stay away from the control of the Civil Aviation Authority.

In general terms I guess it'd be fair to say a number of folk died while the sport of microlighting got to the point it's at now.

The common denominator for both styles of aircraft is the weight. A Microlight is defined as having an empty weight of 268 kilos. i.e. round about the weight of three average sized fellas.

When you add in passengers and fuel the maximum weight is 450 kilos. An extra allowance is made if you have a parachute onboard, which I don't have.

Both types of aircraft seem to use Rotax Engines these days and the manual happily states, all the way through, that the engine isn't certified for aircraft use and is subject to sudden 'stoppages'.

From a flying perspective neither type of Microlight is designed to fly in cloud or can handle icing.

If you find yourself in the fluffy stuff it's very easy to get disorientated and fly head first into the ground.

One poor soul got confused in fog, a couple of years ago, and flew into the Yorkshire Moors. He just didn't realise which way was up or down and smashed into the ground at full throttle. He'll have died quickly but at the same time his head came off.

So not an ideal end to the day.

In terms of the cold, if ice builds up on the wings that changes the aerodynamic shape of the aircraft and you can fall out of the sky.

Hence you can't climb through cloud and neither can you descend through it. The decision process is always under or over, but not through.

Generally both cloud and ice are instrumental to the death of pilots.

One further thing. Microlights don't tend to have 'stall warning horns' so a person's flying needs to be a bit more intuitive than flying a typical light aircraft. Otherwise you'll fall out of the sky and break something. Either you or the aircraft.

My aircraft is a CTSW Microlight. 3 years old. Modern 3 Axis design. Great fun to fly into short farm strips and best of all she has a heater that keeps me relatively warm on winter days.

I absolutely loathe the cold.

Chapter 3 - The Trip

You may have picked up that I'm an adventurer, of sorts.

I initially talked to a few chap's regards flying Round the World as a way of raising money for a Liverpool Cancer Charity I support and having a bloody good adventure at the same time. Check out www.justgiving.com/Jon-Hilton

And in one of life's 'unexpected consequences' the inherent fear of that trip led me to becoming a father. Which is a whole other story. But at the same time it means I have responsibilities.

The Canadian trip seemed like a decent experience. And not an overly long one at that. 7 to 10 days. Not Round the World but not inconsequential and not away from home for too long either. A test.

Having subsequently spoke to a couple of gents about flight clearances I received a pack of instructions and guidance notes through the post. For some reason the paperwork was addressed to a 'Captain Hilton' and I assumed someone had quite rightly assumed I was officer material.

I gave thought to registering the trip with both the Guinness chaps and the FAI folk in France who keep note of flying records. Ultimately I couldn't be bothered.

On four specific occasions I tried to get insurance for the trip. I have life insurance and Search & Rescue cover but no one would insure the aircraft. Bloody pessimists. In the end I thought, sod it, I'll go without.

Decision Height

Why, you might ask, would I risk a £70,000 asset I couldn't afford to replace?

A mixture of two things really. Firstly, I'm an idiot. Secondly, there comes a point when you can't keep making excuses for inactivity. If you make a promise to yourself at some stage you need to follow it through.

One further noteworthy comment that played a part in the decision making was that I'd had a small medical scare. A trip to the optician led to a trip to the hospital. The suggestion being that both eyes were under too much pressure and a train of thought pointed towards a brain tumour saying hello.

It turned out not to be the case, and everything's fine, but that kind of thing focuses the mind a little. Makes you want to get off your behind and experience life before it's too late.

Not being a complete idiot, and as extra peace of mind, a ferry pilot I'd spoken to had volunteered to come with me on the trip. Unfortunately due to his work commitments he'd had to bow out at the last minute. Hence I was forced to ponder the 'go / no go' decision and eventually decided to go alone.

From a logistical perspective I subsequently put the aircraft through an early 200 hour service.

Additionally the radiator grills were partially masked to defeat the cold of the arctic and special antifreeze was added. A further heater modification was added to shunt a little more warmth into the cockpit.

A faulty EGT (Exhaust Gas Temperature) sensor was fixed courtesy of a great chap at London Airsports. He also helped sort out a few calibration issues with the Fuel Flow sensor. Plus the Outside Air Temperature sensor always seemed to under read and he checked into that.

It read correctly at ground level but I felt it was out by about 5 to 10c in the air.

You may have read the last two paragraphs and formed the view the aircraft was falling apart. She wasn't. Just a few items went kaput at the same time.

In terms of navigation kit I couldn't get the maps I wanted on SkyDemon so I was forced to buy another GPS and I opted for the Garmin 795. I also bought another emergency beacon, immersion suit and life raft, plus a range of kit in line with the notes I'd been sent.

At the same time I'd purchased a number of Red shirts so folk could readily spot me or my 'body' from the air. Not a pleasant

Decision Height

consideration but the kind of mortality issue a chap's forced to address.

I'll freely admit to worrying about the lack of insurance but like I said, I guess I'd mentally written off the cost of the aircraft if I broke her.

Last but not least, and somewhat humorously, my local flying school had had a few issues with the Rotax engines powering their Microlights.

Disconcertingly, two of them suffered minor engine failures before I was due to leave and I was on the waiting list for a replacement fuel pump. That type of thing triggers a reality check.

In light of the above I finished off my Will.

Chapter 4 - Basic Terminology

AAIB report; The Air Accident Investigation Branch detail what happens when you crash...

Airfield Circuit; Landing at an airport generally involves flying a rectangular pattern around the airfield.

- **Downwind** is flying parallel to the runway.
- **Base** is 90 degrees to the runway.
- **Final** means you've lined up the runway in the hope of landing. Juggling airspeed and height with the aim of a gentle touchdown, at a certain speed, at a specific point.

Apron; Where you park the aircraft.

Avgas; Fuel for larger aircraft. Not Microlights.

CAVOK; Ceiling & Visibility OK. A very nice day.

Cloud; A bad thing. If you become encased in it you'll likely die. If not you'll definitely need a change of underwear.

Cold; A very bad thing. I don't do 'cold'.

Cruise speed; Approximately 100 knots. Any faster and I burn more fuel than I'd like. The cheapskate in me objects to that. 100 knots isn't far off 2 miles a minute.

Decision Height

CTSW; The aircraft. They have a reputation for being difficult to fly. I'm told that 30% of all CT's in the USA have had some form of crash.

Dynon; The Electronic instrument in the cockpit, sometimes called a Glass Panel, which tells you about altitude, airspeed, temperatures, pressures, etc. There isn't a back up mechanism. Break it & that's it.

Amusingly, when I ordered the aircraft I'd asked that an additional, separate, Compass be added. I assumed the installer would know not to put the magnetic device next to the electrically powered Dynon. He didn't and the additional Compass, which was supposed to represent my peace of mind, is bloody useless in flight.

FBO; The folk at airports who organise things. Fuel, hotels, aircraft parking, logistics. They look after aircraft and aircrew. Usually a necessary expense at larger airports.

Flight plan; For flights of a certain length, especially those that could be considered perilous, you need to complete one. In its simplest form it's so the authorities know where to collect the pilot, or body, in the event of a crash.

Freezing layer; The height at which the temperature turns from positive to negative. ie. cold.

Fuck; Short for, 'oh my lord, what the heck is going on'.

G-CGIZ; Also known as India Zulu. The Registration number given by the Civil Aviation Authority. Folk sometimes take the mickey, for some reason, because of its slightly rude connotations. In my mind it helps give her a personality. She is a she and I've nicknamed her, 'Samson'.

Jon Hilton

IFR; Instrument Flight Rules. For aircraft with more equipment that can fly through cloud. Microlights are not suitable for IFR conditions.

IMC; Instrument & Meteorology Conditions. ie. flying in cloud and poor visibility. If you're not careful disorientation can take effect and you can be upside down without realising it... Folk die in this situation.

Mogas; Car fuel. My Rotax engine is designed to run on it. It can take Avgas for short periods but by preference the engine prefers fuel from garage forecourts such as Shell, BP, Morrisons etc.

OAT; Outside Air Temperature.

OPS; Operations. Where the clever people work. The chaps sat in Towers around the world generally speak English. It's the language of aviation.

Spot GPS; Little round Orange device. Uses Satellites to give folk a 'breadcrumb' view of your travels. Not very reliable. Reassuring little green light on it, though.

Stall; The point the aircraft stops flying and the pilot becomes a passenger. Unless you have a feel for the aircraft your eyes become glued to the Air Speed Indicator to ensure you don't fall out of the sky.

Weather Front; A change in weather conditions. Get decisions wrong regards these blighters and you'll die.

VFR; Visual Flight Rules. You have to be able to see where you're going.

VNE; Velocity Not Exceed. If you fly any faster something will break. Possibly a wing.

And finally as a general observation.... I don't enjoy flying in winds above 10 knots or have visibility of less than 5 miles or have a cloud base less than 2,000 ft. Makes me uncomfortable and a tad claustrophobic.

I like to be able to see where I'm going, not worry about being prematurely forced into the ground, and then land without any dramas at my destination.

Bit of an old scaredy cat really.

Jon Hilton

Chapter 5 - Britain, Faroes, Iceland 24th May

Friday

Barton aerodrome has been around since the 1920's and the Airport Tower is the oldest listed airport structure in the UK. It oozes history in a red brick, functional, fashion.

As an airfield it's just that. Grass runways built on, from what I'm told is, an old land fill site.

Decision Height

That means the runways aren't particularly flat and a great landing can seem like you've completely fucked up as the Barton bumps greet the undercarriage.

The night before the flight I said my goodbyes to my beautiful little daughter and her mum, plus my parents and nieces, and arrived at Barton for 9am. Then proceeded to load my stuff aboard India Zulu.

Very windy day. 20 knots and beyond. Overcast clouds. No one else flying or even thinking about it. I pulled Samson out of the hanger but kept her in the lee of the building. The flags marking the entrance to the Tower building were being thrashed about by the wind.

Jon Hilton

I walked into the reception and started chatting to the young guy on duty. He asked about the trip and if I was really going to do it. For the umpteenth time a voice inside my head screamed at me to go home and have a lie down, but I heard myself say, *'yep, I'm going'*.

My new friend suggested that if I was really heading to a different continent I'd need a mascot. He rooted around under the counter and fished out a small stuffed Santa Claus.

I said it required a personalised name and he suggested 'Wilson' from the Tom Hanks film, Castaway.

In general terms I don't talk to inanimate objects but Wilson looked cheerful and I figured he'd come in useful as a companion.

As an afterthought I asked the young fella to sign a sheet of paper saying I was starting my trip and he was my witness. I also posed for a cheesy, nervous, pic'.

Decision Height

From a flying perspective I was anxious about the winds whistling around outside the building but I signed the departure book with a cheeky, 'Canada via Wick' narrative and slowly walked to the aircraft. I was nervous. I maybe didn't show it, but I was scared.

Samson was on the apron with her wings rocking in the wind. By definition she's a very light aircraft and it's a bad sign when the wind is able to move her around of its own accord.

I quickly climbed aboard and sat there pensively. My weight seemed to make her a tad more grounded. Postpone the trip or keep calm and carry on?

Inside the aircraft I scanned the instruments, stared blankly at all the kit I'd managed to cram on board and generally looked into space.

One of the flying instructors walked past the aircraft and stared at me. A 'you must be mad' look drifted across his face. I kept staring at the wind sock, as it billowed out horizontally, and reluctantly decided to fly.

If I didn't go I'd probably bottle it and never do it.

Shouting *'clear prop'*, as I'd done 500 or so times, I turned the key in the ignition and started the engine. And found myself transfixed by the sight of the prop spinning in front of me. So many things could go wrong.

When the Rotax had warmed up to 50C, and was ready to fly, I radioed the Tower for taxi instructions. *'Runway 02. Circuit left hand. Hold at Charlie 3. QNH pressure setting 1002'* came the reply.

Releasing the brakes, I inched the throttle forward and slowly headed towards the grass taxiway. Without stopping I quickly carried out my power checks and set the flaps and trim. Not

Jon Hilton

normal practice but if I faffed about turning into the wind there was a chance we'd get flipped over. An involuntary frown crept across my forehead.

Holding at Charlie 3 the wind was buffeting India Zulu from behind. Cleared for take-off, I released the brakes, kept the stick towards the gusting wind and quickly rolled onto the runway.

Pushed the throttle fully forward and heard the engine noise increase as we sped across the grass. Airborne almost immediately we rose into the skies like a kite. The wings kept rocking left and right as the conditions simultaneously assaulted the aircraft and bounced me around the cockpit.

With my left hand holding the stick and my right on the throttle I keyed the mike with my thumb and called the Tower. Told them I was changing frequency and took a northerly track towards Scotland.

The wind was slapping against the aircraft as Samson head butted her way through the tumultuous conditions. Each time she took a hit I had to retighten my harness straps as they came loose. I cursed and couldn't help but think that was a bloody poor design.

The headwind was as I'd expected but it reduced my ground speed to 75 knots. Which felt like walking.

The conditions eased off around the Burnley area, my ground speed slowly increased to 100 knots, and I started to feel better.

Almost immediately oppressive looking clouds started to roll in. I was swapping one set of conditions for another.

What the fuck was I doing flying? Feeling twitchy, the decision process was to go on top of the clouds or stay underneath and in sight of the ground. It seemed like I had 1,000ft of terrain

Decision Height

clearance so I stayed under as I flew on towards the Lake District.

I had a quick, nervous, look round the aircraft to make sure everything was secure and all the instruments were in the green. My eye caught the orange 'Spot' Emergency Tracking device. The flashing green LED suggested everything was normal. It didn't feel that way.

The countryside started to eat into my line of sight. My 3 GPS devices were giving me the same information regards my reducing height.

I was being forced lower. Mist was starting to encapsulate the aircraft and I could just make out brown hillsides beneath me.

Not good. Not clever.

Jon Hilton

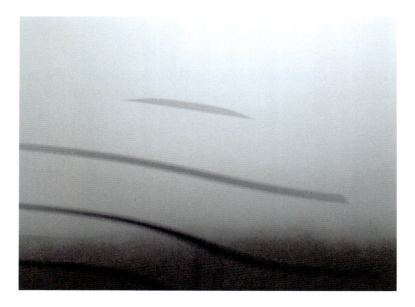

That's the kind of moment when you question your sanity. Nothing to prove to anyone so why proceed? Time to go home.

I moved the stick to the left, kicked in the rudder and banked through 180 degrees. The weather was worse behind me. I was boxed in. Feeling claustrophobic I turned back onto my original track and headed north again. Misty cloud everywhere and lumpy hills underneath me.

The ground looked bloody unforgiving with maybe 500ft of flyable airspace.

All my senses were on full alert. The anxiety was hills, masts or electricity pylons appearing out of the murk in front of me. I was ready to slam the throttle forward, yank the stick back, and charge head first into the cloud. I'd be trading one way of dying for another but ho hum. It wasn't forecast to be this bloody bad for god's sake.

It started raining and water streamed against the windscreen. My focus shortened to watch the individual streaks of rain as

Decision Height

they hit the aircraft. With my stomach churning there was nothing to be done except keep calm. And hope for the best.

The radio crackled and I heard an aircraft talking to Air Traffic. The suggestion was that they'd been caught out by the conditions and were looking for clear skies. The response was that Carlisle would be a good diversion for them to escape the conditions.

That tallied with my reasoning. I was feeling squeezed and pressured but changed from a Northerly course to a more North Westerly track en route to Carlisle Airport.

Scanning the instruments, again, the OAT sensor was reading 2 degrees. Ridiculous for the end of May. The rain had stopped but there was even more haze about. For some reason I swivelled my head left, looked at the wing, and could see ice building. Fuck.

No time to think. I rammed both the stick and throttle forward and dived. The engine roared and my body was forced against the harness straps as we thundered down a valley.

The Dynon began flashing as a warning we were going too fast for the airframe. Amber and Red appeared on the screen. My stomach was churning as I anxiously, repeatedly, checked the condition of each wing.

A couple of mind numbing minutes passed and the mist seemed to retreat a little. I throttled back, alternately scanning the instruments and checking the wings, eyes flicking everywhere. Kept trying to figure my way through various outcomes.

After a further, nervous, five minutes I came out into beautiful clear blue skies. CAVOK territory.

I'm not religious but I'd nearly been born again. That was one of my nine lives used.

Jon Hilton

With my right hand I gently pushed the throttle forward and slowly climbed. Levelling out at 5,000 ft we flew above the clouds on track towards the North East of Scotland.

Bright sunlight streaming through the cabin window above me. Stunning. I could see the remaining ice on the wings turn to water as it fled the flight surfaces.

The warmth of the sun bounced around the cabin and I had a moment of relative cheerfulness. I touched my iPad and it was red hot. A moment later a message popped up, which I didn't catch, and it just stopped working. That was a slap in the face moment... Stay calm, Johnny boy.

The Skydemon software is my preferred source of navigation and a piece of kit I rely on. The need was to get the Garmin 795 programmed so I could make it north without infringing anyone's airspace. I knew how to work the damn thing but it wasn't completely second nature to me.

Decision Height

Reaching forward with my left hand, as I was being lightly bounced about in my seat, I tried to scroll through the various screens and programme in my trip to Wick.

Touch screen devices are nearly bloody impossible to program in flight, because it's so difficult to keep your outstretched finger still, but after much faffing I got it sorted.

The rest of the foray into Scotland was uneventful. The clouds disappeared and there was green everywhere. Beautiful. I flew towards the military base at Lossiemouth and called up their radio frequency to introduce myself and let them know my route.

The lady Air Traffic Controller mentioned that RAF Typhoon jets were doing touch & go's at the airport. She didn't seem perturbed by my presence but I experienced a certain stomach rumbling anxiety. Being near 'military' airspace always makes me twitchy just in case Mr Cockup drops by to say hello.

My worries were unfounded as I made headway north. No drama. No one upset.

Having been airborne for 4 or so hours I found myself over the Forth of Fife and experienced a certain unpleasantness at being over the tiny stretch of water. That didn't bode well.

I latterly joined left base for Wick airport and landed. The sun was shining on the Scots. Feeling very drained I got out of the aircraft and tried to stretch away the days exertions.

Two American chaps came over to say hi. They were flying the Atlantic in a corporate jet. One slim and thirties. The other was older and I guessed the aircraft owner.

They asked what I was doing and I mentioned Canada. *'You're brave'*, came the reply. I shrugged and said, *'I feel bloody stupid for taking on the trip'*.

Jon Hilton

The refuelling truck trundled over, stopped, and I filled up with Avgas. Not ideal fuel for the Rotax Engine but she'd have to get used to it for a while.

I climbed back into the cabin and sat inside the aircraft, one leg in, the other dangling outside and checked the fuel consumption on the Dynon against the actual fuel burn. The figures didn't match. The suggestion was that I'd landed with 15 litres more than I'd got. Bugger.

Fifteen litres is nearly an hours' flight time. Believing you've got more fuel on board than you actually have can lead to unhealthy decisions. A potentially life threatening discrepancy.

I'd been safe and still had a decent reserve but my OCD hates it when any numbers don't tally up. My stomach tightened as I started scrolling through the unfamiliar settings screen on the Dynon to tweak the calibration numbers.

I damn well needed the fuel readings to be correct so I could have an element of certainty about the point the prop' would stop spinning.

Having tweaked the numbers, on a DOS type admin screen, I vowed never to fiddle with the management settings again.

Then shut the system down, got out of the aircraft, and wandered over to one of the buildings. Made my way up the old staircase, and introduced myself to the guy in OPS.

Pleasant guy, friendly.

We looked at the weather together. There was a weak front passing between Scotland and the Faroes and that gave me a moment of reflection.

As a rule it's bad form to fly through weather fronts. The chap suggested it wouldn't be too bad. He knew I was VFR only and I figured I could turn round if it was a problem. That's what I hoped. Three hour flight. Seven hours of endurance.

There was a feeling of anxiety inside me, though. Weather can be unpredictable. I knew I'd be out to sea for hours and I tried to mentally run through my ditching drills so I'd be prepared for a crash landing in the sea. An unsettling train of thought.

Wick to the Vagar, Faroe Islands.

Returning to Samson with half a dozen Mars bars I slipped into the lower half of my immersion suit, got airborne, and flew past the Orkneys.

Jon Hilton

I spotted a nifty looking rock formation and, without thinking about it, shut the throttle and dropped from 3,000 feet to 300 feet to have a gander at an Old Man of Hoy type feature.

Feeling silly but with my curiosity satisfied, I pushed the throttle forward and climbed again en route towards Vagar.

A low throbbing noise started to permeate through the headset and I realised the lack of any other radio chatter meant all I could hear was the heartbeat of the engine.

The weather was fine. Fairly low cloud but the visibility was great and in line with what I'd expected.

Decision Height

With my left hand on the stick I used my right to reach into my rucksack, on the passenger seat, and root around. By touch I felt the file of papers I'd printed off before the trip and pulled it out. Revision needed.

Two and a half hours later I was dinking around a few islands to find the airport.

Reaching forward I tried to flip through the screens on the Garmin 795 to show the view that gave a 3D representation of the aircraft and the surrounding topography. The logic being that it shows the aircraft's position relative to the sides of the fjord.

Jon Hilton

The page appeared and within 20 seconds I decided it was a bloody useless feature that had been created for the benefit of Garmin's marketing efforts. No use to me and just a distraction. I switched back to the standard map view.

Vagar Airport has a long runway. Big enough for the occasional Airbus but it's not flat. They've built it on the crest of a hill and there's a high peak on one side. I had anxieties about mucky, turbulent air cascading over the hill and causing problems.

The CT is a very light aircraft and disturbed air can affect its ability to fly straight and level. Worst case would mean a crash landing.

I called Air Traffic and was cleared for a straight-in approach. No buggering about with circuits. Simply follow the fjord and land. Water underneath me, hills either side, cloud above me.

Decision Height

On finals I could see the runway lights extending from the hump of the runway into the sea. The landing lights are on stilts maybe 30m above ground level.

I should have been straight onto the runway but the tourist in me couldn't help but slow the aircraft down and make a slalom manoeuvre around the last hundred meters or so to check out the runway lights.

Jon Hilton

Feeling like a dick for playing the Karl Pilkington role (an Idiot Abroad) I got my act together and flew along the centreline of the runway.

I touched down at 50 knots. Gently dabbed the brakes and slowed to walking pace, taxied to the apron, shut the engine down and sat there staring into space.

A fuel wagon drove up to the aircraft and a skinny middle aged chap got out.

I climbed out of India Zulu and said hi. He looked at Samson and appeared a little confused. We reached a nearly wordless understanding that I didn't need Jet fuel, the silly sod, and that Avgas would do.

Decision Height

Walking to each wing, I reached up and unscrewed the fuel caps. The fella got a pair of step ladders and climbed up with the fuel hose in hand ready to fuel the left tank.

I turned away and wandered off for a moment checking out the buildings and generally looking around. When I turned back, he was on the top step, fuel hose between his legs, the fuel cap off, and was making a phone call.

It's in the Air Navigation Order that you can't use a phone near fuel vapours in case there's an explosion. Maybe he'd missed the memo. I stared at him, in a state of jaded disbelief, hoping he wouldn't get his Old Holborn out and roll a fag.

To add insult to injury the bugger managed to slosh fuel all over the wings as he topped up the tanks. And that pissed me off no end.

I simply smiled at him and mentally wished him the pox.

Jon Hilton

After cleaning the excess fuel from the flight surfaces, with my sponge, I walked to the Tower, climbed the stairs, and met the lady running OPS. She seemed friendly, not to mention a little bored, and we chatted a little. I asked for the weather and said I might fly on to Iceland that evening. The report seemed ok. Not great, but do-able. Similar to what I'd flown through.

At the same time she handed me a pamphlet that listed dozens and dozens of weather symbols and codes. The document was printed by the Danish CAA who control the Greenlandic and Faroe skies.

I'd brought a few flying books with me, for reference, but the paperwork she'd passed me seemed specifically designed for flying the North Atlantic. Very intimidating stuff and I felt sick to my stomach that I'd no clue what some of it meant.

The lady helped me create the flight plan, signed my sheet of paper, and I very slowly made my way back to the aircraft. Got out my immersion suit and half struggled into it.

As an incidental comment, I bought the bugger from a pilot supplies shop. It's impossible to wear. It's an all-inclusive beast so your hands are all part of the suit and you can't write with it on or use the radio. So I fly with it half on and half off. The logic being that when the engine fails I'm at a safe altitude and have time to fully get into it and zip it up.

Vagar to Reykjavik, Iceland.

Fifteen minutes later I taxied out, lined up, and took off. Maybe 7pm by then. Heading to Reykjavik. The smell of aircraft fuel, courtesy of my wing cleaning duties, was beginning to have an impact. A feeling of tiredness started to wash over me knowing I'd need to be alert for another 3 or so hours.

It started to rain and steady streams of water hit the aircraft. It covered the windscreen like a waterfall. I looked at the wings

Decision Height

and could see individual streaks of water careering across the surface.

Feeling both claustrophobic and vulnerable I was presented with a bank of cloud again. I shook my head and under my breath said, 'go fuck yourself'.

Decision needed. Under or over? I reluctantly pushed the stick forward and tried under. Nothing to see except the ocean and clouds with a narrow gap for me to fly through. Felt thoroughly alone.

Realisation dawned that I was in a battle to stay alive and I began to feel queasy.

The cloud base was 2,000ft, then it became a 1,000ft. Then 500ft. At the lowest point I was rushing along a couple of hundred feet above the frigidly cold and deathly waters of the North Atlantic.

A thick covering of clouds just above my head, the sight of individual waves below me, and a palpable feeling of anxiety in my stomach.

I needed to be higher and have more breathing space between me and the Ocean.

A hole appeared in the cloud, I forced the throttle forward and started a climbing turn to the left. Like a helter-skelter ride I kept turning, and turning, through 360 degrees as I fought for height. After ten minutes I came out on top of the cloud at about 6,000 ft.

Crystal blue skies above me, but it felt cold.

Jon Hilton

With my right hand I grabbed my folder of notes, which was neatly wedged behind my large rucksack on the passenger seat. Single-handedly leafing through the pages I tried to memorise various frequencies. Then keyed the mike and started making radio calls.

On the third attempt I made contact with the Icelandic controller. Gave my position report and asked about the winds and conditions at my destination airport only to be told they'd changed from the forecast weather. Surprise, surprise they'd deteriorated.

I asked about my alternate destination and that seemed better. 15knots, 5,500ft cloud base. Decision needed. No brainer really, I changed my flight plan over the radio, passed over my latitude and longitude, and headed north to Akureyri.

About 50 miles out the clouds descended and Samson and I followed suit. My Garmin showed the jagged nature of the headland. Worryingly there were splashes of red that meant I

Decision Height

was too low to follow a direct route to the airport without hitting something pointy.

Flying higher wasn't an option without hitting more clouds, so I decided to take a trek around the coast and find a way inland after the mountains had fallen away.

Trapped between the sea and different levels of cloud. I had an unhealthy feeling I'd get squeezed into submission and have to turn back.

The weather cleared up. Visibility was great. Iceland's mountain's came into view and I headed inland. Desolate countryside. Lots of snow. Beautiful from a, 'I'm relying on one engine to keep me alive', perspective.

Jon Hilton

If the engine failed my Kendal Mint Cake would be useless in Iceland's volcanic, snow covered flatlands.

A bloody big lump of a mountain appeared on my left and before I realised what I was doing I'd changed course to have a gander. It looked like a frosted hot cross bun sat on a plate. Or a lady's breast.

At the point I was within touching distance, and had had a decent gawp, it struck me that I was miles off course and if there was a problem I might not get rescued if the search and rescue chaps didn't allow for me being a bloody idiot. I decided to stop being a dickhead tourist and get back on track.

Annoyed with myself I kept scanning the instruments and tried to suppress my growing unease. At the same time I was trying to study all the weather information and airport data I'd brought with me. Papers were scattered everywhere around the cabin.

I'd always appreciated the trip was dangerous. I knew that no matter what I read, whilst in England, the flight would lead to a greater need for knowledge. Flying, scanning the instruments, trying to study was mentally draining. The smell of fuel wasn't helping.

Approaching the airfield I changed frequencies and asked for the weather at the airport. The cloud base had dropped and the wind was now gusting beyond 25 knots. Fifteen knots faster than I would have preferred.

The view outside the cockpit was deceptively beautiful with statuesque clouds and mountains galore.

The reality of clipping the white stuff would mean more icing issues. Flying too low could mean getting caught in winds that would flip me over. Both potentially deadly.

Looking in the general direction of the airport I could see mountains and bloody big hills with clouds loitering above them. I'd have to thread the aircraft through slivers of clear sky to reach safety.

The thought went through my mind that I seriously should have spent more time trying to get insurance. There wasn't sufficient fuel or time to divert elsewhere. Push on or crash land seemed the two options on offer.

I crested a line of snow covered hills with 100ft to spare between me, the clouds, and the ground. A second later the bloody big runway, in the centre of the valley, came into view.

It tallied with the satellite imagery I'd got and that made me feel a tad better.

Feeling in awe of everything I began asking, "What the fuck was a fool like me doing in Iceland?"

I joined left base, cursing at the weather gods, and with the controllers blessing, lined up on final approach.

The weather gods were trying to keep the aircraft aloft and like a kite on a string she took an age to come down. We slowly advanced to the runway threshold. I floated her along the centreline and India Zulu tentatively, reluctantly, settled to earth.

We taxied off the runway and, with the aircraft no longer facing into wind, the wings started rocking. Not pleasant. The wind howled and tried to flip us over.

It was 10pm by then and I'd completed 10 hours of flying. I was now both knackered and numb to any potential accident. Nothing was going to kill me tonight.

Over the radio we were directed to a parking area, away from the runway, where I shut the aircraft down and got out. Without my weight onboard she immediately started to move around. The wind was slapping against her and she was trying to weather vane in the direction of the gusts. Not healthy.

Jon Hilton

I jumped back aboard I switched the Master on, called the Tower and asked for somewhere indoors to park. They said there was nothing available. Nothing to tie down to either.

She wouldn't survive the night in this wind. In the morning I'd find a jumble of composite and carbon fibre wrapped round a building. The only option would be to sleep in the aircraft cabin and hope my lardy butt kept her grounded. Then hope for the best as night became day.

I was staring blankly in front of me and in my peripheral vision spied a couple of guys moving around near one of the hangers. It was late in the evening and I was worried about everyone buggering off home, so I urgently gestured for them to come over.

Through a mixture of my pointing to the moving wings, shaking my head and shrugging, I got my point across that there was a problem.

I silently cursed that it wasn't compulsory that everyone, everywhere, speak fluent English.

My new friends pointed to a hangar. It was more of a utility space where the airport snow plough was kept. Grabbing hold of the prop' I started pulling the aircraft towards safety.

In return the chaps started to take over, which was such a bloody relief. Two of them reached out for a propeller blade to help her along. It's a three bladed affair and I felt like I was in the way so I let go and turned to face the wind. If I'd had hair it'd have been blown all over the place.

The aircraft wouldn't fit straight in to the building but somehow the chaps managed to shoehorn her inside whilst I tried not to fall asleep standing up.

Decision Height

Four incredibly helpful guys. Out of the gusting conditions I felt she was safe.

The fellas seemed to have taken to me and one of the chaps generously drove me to town and helped organise a smart looking hostel. 11pm by then.

Akureyri has a population of 16,000 people and it seemed to me that a hefty proportion lot of them were out and about socialising. Some were drunk and being sick on the pavements. Being from Bolton, I felt somewhat at home but it's a tad disconcerting when it's broad daylight, mind.

Found a Subway type outlet and had a sandwich. Drank a beer at the hostel bar, while a rock band played, and made it to bed by 12pm.

Absolutely cream crackered.

Jon Hilton

Decision Height

Chapter 6 - Iceland, Greenland 25th May

Saturday

Reluctantly opened my eyes at 5am as light streamed through the flimsy curtains. Cursing, I got out of bed to see if I could adjust the fabric in some way and reintroduce darkness into the room. No bloody chance, it wasn't happening.

Not pleased with the world I walked to the bathroom, showered and put on another red thermal shirt. Red isn't my colour and the logic behind wearing it is enough to put a chap off his toast.

43

Jon Hilton

Walked the mile or two from the hostel to the provincial airport. Lugging my rucksack over one shoulder and the much larger seaman's bag over the other. Overcast day. Pretty windy, again. 20knots, plus.

The conifer type trees, along the pathway, were bending in the wind and a lady jogged past me. It felt cold and I considered running to keep warm but then thought, 'sod that for a game of soldiers'.

A chilly thirty minutes later I arrived at the airport and started faffing about trying to find and check the available weather information for a flight from Iceland to Greenland.

There was another weather front in the way but it looked like it was dying out. Broken cloud at 5,000ft around my destination. Everywhere looked worse for tomorrow.

I found a local pilot, discussed the route, and he thought today was the best day to fly. Checked with a friend in England and he agreed. I was struggling with a few anxieties but chose to put them out of my mind.

The pilot I'd spoken to, very friendly chap called Birkir, drove me to the local petrol station to buy unleaded fuel and haul it back to the Airport in his jerry cans.

Back on site, with Birkir's help, I found another computer terminal and started re-reading all the data I'd viewed an hour earlier. Winds, pressure readings, temperatures, conditions at Kulusuk. Differing timeframes and satellite images flashed in front of me and I could feel myself constantly frowning.

My thoughts were that the trip was do-able but I felt the need to ask for another opinion. From one of the buildings on the airport complex I phoned up the guy in the Tower to ask his advice.

He thought the flight should be fine. Colourful chap. Instantly likeable. He even threw in a few light-hearted anecdotes about his ancestors.

Apparently the term, 'writing on the wall', dates back to the Vikings killing their enemies and then writing messages in their blood. Not quite what I was expecting to hear when asking for advice about the weather but I played along.

I paid my landing fees, plus some sort of customs levy, and sat amongst the passengers in the departure lounge as they waited for a commercial flight to Reykjavik. I started 'people watching' and began wondering what their lives were like.

My gaze fell on a large turbo prop aircraft, sitting 30ft from me, and wondered how warm it'd be on board and if there'd be a hostess service or toilet. I leafed through my various bits of paper, munched on a Mars bar, and was envious of those drinking tea.

Then I questioned my sanity again and felt numb all over. What a complete and utter fuckwit. Why was I doing this?

The fellas I'd met the other day appeared and latterly helped me jiggle India Zulu backwards and forwards to get her out of the maintenance hangar. They seemed to take the view I was an eccentric Brit to be applauded for trying something stupid.

Very friendly lot.

Jon Hilton

Birkir and the chaps helped me fuel Samson. I got my piece of paper signed, struggled into my immersion suit, or at least half of it, and said my goodbyes to the guys.

Climbing aboard the aircraft I strapped my two bags to the passenger seat, switched on the Master and set about checking the fuel burn figures again. They were still out of whack with Samson's actual consumption. I flicked through the Dynon screens to find the settings page where I could adjust the calculation mechanism, again, and hopefully narrow the gap.

Not for the first time the thought went through my mind, 'do not fuck up any other settings whilst fiddling with this bloody thing'.

Then I tried to put all doubts from my mind, put the key in the ignition, called *'clear prop'*, and started the engine. With the propeller spinning I warmed the Rotax in the lee of one of the buildings.

Decision Height

Keying the mike I spoke to the Tower, copied down the runway, taxi instructions, pressure settings and asked for an immediate departure.

Released the brakes and taxied beyond the shelter of the hangers into the full force of the wind. She started rocking. Feeling edgy I held her steady, rolled onto the runway and took off.

We began putting distance between us and the airport as we flew along the length of the valley. Getting ready to change radio frequencies my chatty friend in the Tower chirped up and volunteered, *'there's a lot of blue sky to the west'*.

My plan had been to go north, hit the coast, stay below the cloud, then head west by flying around the headland. His suggestion meant a shorter flight time and that seemed an attractive proposition. I thanked him, gently applied full power, and started a climbing turn to the left.

A little bit of crystal blue appeared in between the overcast clouds and that improved my mood. Beautiful panorama. Snow covered mountains everywhere. Lots of solid fluffy cloud.

Picture postcard stuff.

Moments later the temperature started dropping and I found myself boxed in by both mountain peaks and ice laden clouds.

Still an access hole above me into the most amazing blue but full power wasn't giving me the rate of climb I was hoping for. India Zulu kept circling through 360 degrees as we fought for height.

Jon Hilton

I could see stunningly azure skies above me but we were surrounded by thick white pockets of freezing water vapour. My insides started churning.

The hole I'd been climbing through started to close like a trap. One wing clipped the edge of a cloud and instantly ice crystals appeared on the carbon fibre surfaces and windscreen. My head was swivelling left and right trying to assess the impact of the ice build-up. I urged her upwards.

India Zulu's flight characteristics started to change and, as if drunk, she became sluggish. She wouldn't climb any higher and we levelled out at 7,000ft. Nothing I could do. I was becoming a passenger instead of the pilot.

White Mountain peaks just visible below me but no viable emergency landing spot.

I realised the only way was down.

Decision Height

Instant life and death decision required. I figured I was goosed either way. Stay high, collect more ice, then just drop out of the sky and die. Or dive straight down and shake off a bit of the cold stuff before the wings broke loose and I died.

Eyes frantically scanning everywhere I spotted a valley, and rammed both the stick and throttle forward. She dropped like a stone. Passed Samson's VNE speed. Aircraft noise increasing. Instruments going red. Ears popping. I felt the G-force through my whole body.

Couldn't help but wonder which part of the airframe would fail first. Which wing would buckle and what I would actually feel when I hit the snow and rocks in the valley floor.

Every muscle clenched. Constantly flicking my eyes from the instruments to the wings and then scanning for a flat place to crash. For 100 or so incredibly long seconds I sat on the knife edge of what the aircraft could take.

Everything held together. She started to fly more like her old self. Thank fuck-a-doodle-do for German engineering.

I throttled back before the engine cylinders cracked, and ran along the valley floor at a couple of hundred feet, aiming for the coast. White everywhere outside the cabin. The airspeed slowed to normal cruise and the instruments returned to green.

Mentally I was going through the "dead man walking" stage and cursed myself for listening to the Tower chap. He didn't know my aircraft and what she was capable of. He was trying to be helpful but listening to him had nearly killed me.

Reaching the sea I followed the jagged cliffs around the headland. Streams of water became visible under each wing as the ice dissipated and fled. Areas of blue sky above me.

Jon Hilton

The weather turned again.

Specks of sleet started hitting the windscreen. Not sticking though. Hypnotic. Less than a mile visibility. Maybe half that.

Decision Height

No chance of getting fully into the immersion suit if the rubber band at the front failed.

Seeing jagged cliff faces and inlets, that few folk have ever seen, Samson flew at round about 100ft above the North Atlantic.

My insides were in turmoil. Anxious, scared, worried but surprisingly resigned to matters at the same time.

For some reason I started to think of ex-girlfriends and wondered how I'd got to this moment in my life. A sobering period of contemplation. Meaning of life stuff.

How would Ava grow up without me? Would she be better or worse off?

I was concentrating on flying but just couldn't help my thoughts shifting and I wondered if that's what happened just before you die.

A 100ft above the sea at 110 miles per hour meant any momentary lapse in concentration would mean I'd become an ex human being. Humorously the Monty Python Parrot sketch flickered through my mind and that cheered me up a little.

For 45 minutes my left hand was firmly attached to the stick and my right hand was glued to the throttle lever. The sleet hitting both the windscreen and wings felt like a bloody nightmare come real.

No radio contact with anyone. Thoroughly alone. Constantly praying the conditions wouldn't deteriorate further.

Jon Hilton

The weather cleared up, scraps of blue on show, and we climbed to relative safety. At 2,000ft I felt sufficiently secure to delve into my stash of Mars bars.

An hour later another wall of dense cloud appeared. My heart sank. Under or over. I'd had my fill of the fucking sea, pardon my French, so we climbed and kept climbing.

The clouds drew closer and I put India Zulu into a spiralling climb. Round and round and round we went whilst gaining height.

I glanced at the Dynon and found it wasn't happy. The Airspeed Indicator suggested Samson was doing up to 400 knots. That had to be wrong or I'd have lost the wings already.

The instruments were suggesting we were also facing a 99 knot headwind. Surely that couldn't be right. Could it?

Decision Height

I levelled out to try and think my way through the situation. The Artificial Horizon was still suggesting I was in a 60 degree banking turn... but as far as I was aware we were flying straight and level.

Fuck it, either I'm faulty or the instruments are. Not turning back. Without realising it I found myself unwrapping another Mars.

Trying to give myself time to think I started a slow turn through 360 degrees. No guarantee things would be easier heading back. At Kulusuk the weather would be good. Akureyri had been unpleasant.

Reluctantly, with my butt muscles clenching, I turned back on course to Greenland.

A bank of clouds, like a floating brick wall, glared at me and I found myself staring up at them hoping I could claw my way on top. Scowling and shaking my head I began running my right hand across my brow.

Jon Hilton

Samson slowly climbed up to a mammoth 12,500ft and we skimmed above a carpet of white stuff on route to Kulusuk. I was keenly aware of needing additional oxygen at this height.

It was minus ridiculously cold. I'd taken to subtracting 10 degrees from the OAT sensor readings. With that logic it was possibly 20 below freezing within inches of my head and torso.

My eyes were glued to the engine temperatures. I needed to keep the Rotax warm and the instruments in the green even if that meant pushing her harder than seemed sensible. That would increase my fuel burn but my earlier calculations had already gone out of the window. It might be tight.

I was pondering the meaning of life and simultaneously looking at two sets of instruments, air speed and horizon, that were blatantly wrong.

Was I in a banked turn facing a 99 knot headwind? What was my airspeed? Were the instruments faulty? I started to second guess everything.

There was a period of calm rationalisation as I tried to figure out whether I was getting hypoxia or generally having a breakdown.

I glanced at my finger nails to see whether altitude sickness was kicking in and check if they'd started turning blue. I didn't think they were, but I'm a tiny bit colour blind and couldn't help wonder whether the shade that denoted hypoxia was visible to me or not.

A stabbing pain shot through my knee. The heavy mounting mechanism that held my Garmin 795 to the window had broken loose. A hell of a bloody shock. Too cold for it to stay attached to the Plexiglass, it'd just fallen off and hit me. I felt the pain but more than that, I felt alone.

Decision Height

I clumsily tried to reattach it to the window. That was now my primary navaid and it needed to be exactly where it'd been. My fingers were frigidly cold but after half a dozen attempts I finally managed to remount it.

If we were engulfed in cloud, and crashed, no one would know where to find me. Still no radio contact with another living soul. Twelve thousand feet or so of dense cloud less than 20ft from my wheels. Beautiful but deadly. She couldn't climb any higher and we were at the absolute limit of what Samson could handle.

Whilst fumbling with the Garmin I'd wandered off course and now turned back on track. And decided that if there was a hole in the cloud I'd rather be lower. I'd had my fill of being at bloody altitude. Too cold. Too intense. Too isolated. Too much of a knife edge.

If I went any further distance and subsequently got eaten up by rising clouds, because India Zulu couldn't climb above them, I'd be a gonner. The airframe would get iced over, I'd become disorientated and the engine would get too cold... Game over.

For some reason I felt myself simultaneously grimace and heard myself laugh out loud as I reasoned through that train of thought.

Then reached for my iPhone. It had an artificial horizon function on it that I'd bought for less than a pound at the App Store. Zeroing it against the horizon I reached forward with my right hand to adjust the Garmin 495.

That Garmin was just a backup for longitude and latitude fixes, but it did have a page that showed whether we were in level flight or not.

I didn't want to go fully IMC and become encased in cloud, but felt mentally prepared for it. Life or death. My Insides were twisting themselves in knots.

Jon Hilton

Ten minutes later I spotted what looked like a misty hole in the cloud. I shook my head, took a deep breath, and dived and dived and dived. Stomach muscles tightening. Noise increasing. Ears popping. Forced against the harness straps my eyes were fixed on the instruments.

Outside the aircraft all I could see was mist, a whiteout situation. Minutes passed. I knew we'd be accumulating ice. Then the blue of the ocean started to become visible. Misty blue at first, then a deeper navy colour.

I pulled back on the stick and a massive wave of relief hit me as Samson responded to my requests by shallowing out of our dive. We'd be ice laden but we weren't beat.

At a thousand feet there was nothing to see except water and cloud. Both were too bloody close for comfort. I was alive, though.

Staring at the left hand wing I could see a sheen of ice. There were bulkier deposits in between the wing and flaps. Over the course of twenty minutes the ice slowly dissipated.

Depressingly, the cloud base deteriorated and I thought, 'here we go again'. I found myself at a couple hundred feet, listening to the throb of the engine and staring at the waves, wondering when my luck would run out.

Another cat's life had just meowed bye bye.

For good measure I tried to put my arms fully inside the immersion suit. Couldn't manage it. The sleeves were wedged behind me. Every time I moved position to get into the suit the aircraft started to move out of control.

Figured by the time anyone got to me, even with the immersion suit on, I'd be dead anyway. So I thought fuck it, leave it off.

Decision Height

I heard jet pilots on the radio and started making RT transmissions, but no one was picking up my calls. After repeated effort I managed to contact a jet, 30,000ft or so higher and relayed my latitudes and longitudes. They were going to pass on my location to the authorities. I didn't feel very reassured but having spoken to "someone" I felt better.

Five minutes later the weather cleared and I climbed to what seemed like a healthy 5,000ft. I spotted a fishing boat below and descended to have a look. My first sight of anyone in hours.

On the basis of my increasing anxiety levels I gave serious consideration to ditching and sailing home with them. Dipping a wing, Samson started circling.

I'd put thought into ditching in the sea before leaving Blighty. But in reality the idea of a gentle descent, with a subtle splash down, then trying to climb out of the cabin with the life raft in hand didn't seem plausible.

Jon Hilton

No matter how I judged the touch down into the ocean I'd be thrown forward violently. Vicious, freezing, water would fill the cabin. I wouldn't be able to get the life raft out in time and there was a real doubt whether I'd be able to get into the immersion suit.

With a low wing aircraft it might be doable. With Samson's high wing configuration I'd be screwed. Time wouldn't be on my side. No matter how calm or unflappable I was, I wouldn't survive.

A commercial pilot friend of mine had suggested taking a gun with me in case the engine failed. The joke being that it'd be a simpler, quicker, solution to shoot myself rather than go through a lingering death. The definition of lingering being a minute or so in the sea.

I reluctantly stopped orbiting the vessel, unwrapped another Mars and continued westward.

An hour later small pieces of ice began peppering the ocean. White against dark blue. Then more ice. Then small icebergs. Then sheet ice stretching for miles.

Feeling both queasy and cold I reached out with my right hand to pull open the heater control and try to shunt a bit more warmth into the cabin.

A vision of carrying out an emergency landing on the ice seemed like a doer if things went tits up. Then another vision of being eaten by a polar bear came to mind. Yet again I didn't think I'd survive the landing so I tried to put both out of my mind.

I cast around for other things to think about, as a distraction, and started trying to guess my fuel consumption stats. Incredibly drained I started trying to figure out the maths.

Having repeatedly climbed at full power and then dived at VNE I was asking myself the extent to which the Dynon's fuel readings went out of the window. I was reasonably sure of the device, after I'd reset it, but there's nothing hugely reassuring about anything whilst you're over the North Atlantic. Flying off course wouldn't have helped conserve fuel.

If I missed my destination through lack of fuel or poor weather that would be that. No chance of diverting to any other airport in Greenland if the conditions went tits up.

The clouds came down and I descended towards sea level. Kulusuk had forecast decent weather but this seemed to be a glitch. I was spotting icebergs and having to fly around them.

I couldn't help myself and kept heading off course to look at the bigger chunks. Dickhead tourist again.

So tired.

Jon Hilton

Thirty minutes later, after repeated radio calls, I finally picked up the Greenland Information frequency and managed to speak to a fellow human being.

A crisp voice, in English, asked for my 'lats & longs' and ETA for Kulusuk. Civilisation beckoned.

Twenty'ish miles out I was swapped onto the Kulusuk frequency. I called three times without reply.

That drains a person, but I finally got an answer. The weather forecast, at my arrival time, had been a 5,500ft ceiling and good visibility. Typically what you might think of as a nice day and something I was bloody looking forward too.

The coastline materialised in front of India Zulu. I felt relieved, but that bought a new set of headaches. The mountain tops seemed obscured in mist with cloud at 600ft. Visibility of less than a mile. A creamy look to everything. An unhealthy situation.

Decision Height

Over the radio, the Kulusuk Air Traffic chap informed me of the runway length, its gravel status, and that there were snow banks on either side of the runway. For good measure there was water running across it, he said.

My lack of insurance came to mind. No pressure, Johnny boy.

Flying straight in from the ocean side of the airport I started to feel mildly better at being over solid ground. Not safe yet.

Even though the airport was only a mile or so away I couldn't see it. Everything looked frozen with evil haze obscuring my view. Made a right turn and flew along the centre of the valley towards what I hoped was the runway.

Air Traffic cleared me for final approach and landing. The Danish sounding fella seemed very official. He made several further comments about the pressure settings and winds but I started to fade out his voice and focus on flying the aircraft.

I tried to reply to his comments in a professional manner but I think we both knew I wasn't really paying attention. Aviate, Navigate and lastly Communicate was the mantra.

In simple terms that meant putting my brain into neutral and trying to absorb whatever I could. The feel of the aircraft, the wind against her, the visibility, the surroundings and what he'd said.

A gravel runway would be a first and that brought the potential for punctures. How big would the stones be? How much trouble would any patches of water cause? How near to the runway were the ice banks?

Just fly the aircraft you fucking moron and do your best.

A grey streak appeared in front of me. I had the airport satellite image in mind but the snow, cloud, and definition of the valley

Jon Hilton

sides made it look bugger all like its' picture. The dirt line was the runway.

Pulling the throttle back, and slowing, it dawned on me that the Air Speed Indicator had packed up. Too much water in the pitot tube and the freezing conditions had done for that piece of kit.

I'd have to guess my landing speeds by the feel of the aircraft and try not to screw up.

The snow banks alongside the runway came into focus. I floated her over the threshold marker, gently touched down, slowed and then stopped. I could feel the gravel through the wheels as I back tracked the runway.

Decision Height

Bloody relieved I taxied off the active and parked. Switching off the Master, I took the key out of the ignition and sat there for 5 minutes, or so, just staring into space.

Looking blankly at the instruments I absently switched through the screens on the Dynon and it suggested there was 25 litres of fuel reserve remaining in the tanks. Just over half a Jerry Tanks worth in each wing.

I struggled out of the gull wing door and stretched away nearly 6 hours of flying. Then slowly peeled off the lower half of my immersion suit, which had become more like 'leggings' at this point.

A young native type appeared by the side of the aircraft. The first thing I asked the fella was the difference between the

Jon Hilton

weather forecast and the actual conditions. He said, *'the weather changes very quickly round here. I wouldn't rely on the forecasts if I were you'*..... I swore out loud and then apologised for my language.

Walking over to the Tower with my new friend, we started chatting. He said it was a lovely aircraft. I agreed. I was damn tired but not to such an extent to be grumpy.

He wanted to make small talk so I went along with the conversation. We discussed where he'd been in the United States, where he'd gone to school and why he'd come back to Greenland.

I wasn't really listening but being polite doesn't cost anything.

We walked into the building, climbed a set of spiral stairs and emerged into the Tower. He introduced me to a Danish chap called Jesper who appeared to be in charge. All very pleasant.

The new guy seemed happy. Good looking fella. He seemed pleasant and I asked that he check my flight plan was closed. Everyone was smiling.

He looked out the window at Samson, took a drag on his roll up cigarette, looked a little sheepish and asked about the aircraft's weight.

The international code for the aircraft is FDCT and that's what I'd put on the flight plan. That covers the aircraft up to 600kg. On all other paperwork I'd put 450kg. So, I said 450kg.

He scribbled that down. Then said, *'we don't allow Ultralights into Greenland unless they've been bought through Denmark'.*

I said, *'oh?'*

Decision Height

There was nothing to be done at that point. I was absolutely shagged and could hardly string a sentence together.

The airfield was about to close. It was Sunday the following day and Greenland closes down for the day. I said, *'I'm sure we can sort things out and by the way where's the hotel please?'*

I had the specific impression I'd been suckered into saying the aircraft's weight. The flight, all 5.9 hours of it, had been a bugger and I hadn't been on the defence against additional bureaucracy when I landed.

The hotel was two minutes away by car. More of a lodge than anything else. It was set up as a Polar Experience with 20 or so rooms and it had only 2 guests. One of whom was going to be me.

The season for tourists gawping at polar bears hadn't started yet and the staff were pretty much invisible. I felt like an arctic Robinson Crusoe.

I was told by the receptionist that a polar bear was marauding around the village. I was also told it was usually warmer at this time of the year.

Neither point helped improve my outlook on life.

Jon Hilton

Kulusuk has a population of 300 folk. No pub.

Decision Height

Chapter 7 - Greenland 26th May

Sunday

I woke up at 5am in a slightly tacky hotel room. Really thin curtains meant my eyes were being assaulted by daylight.

There was a second single bed, on the other side of the room, and I crawled across the 4ft divide to grab hold of the other duvet. I slithered back into bed and pulled it over my head in a bloody fruitless attempt at blocking out the light.

By 7am I was showered and ready for breakfast. After a selection of toast and cold meats I walked downstairs and had a look outside the hotel.

Jon Hilton

A beat up car was parked up immediately in front of the doorway. Snow and ice everywhere with a sky blue canopy dotted with cotton wool clouds.

Feeling ridiculously tired I trudged along the half mile road to the airport. Walls of ice 10ft tall framed the thoroughfare as if I was in a bloody big trench.

Couldn't help looking upwards and wonder if there was a damn big man eating polar bear wandering around trying to sniff out the blood of an Englishman.

The thought of being eaten alive and then crapped out through the butt hole of a big white predator, added a little spice to my walk. It'd be ironic if I'd travelled all this distance to be an all you can eat buffet.

To take my mind off matters I set about etching a little bit of graffiti into the vertical sides of the road. Dad had been suffering with a heart complaint and I etched the old buggers

Decision Height

name into the hillside. I walked on towards the airport wondering whether it'd melt or be there for a hundred years.

At the airport I had a quick look at India Zulu to check she was still upright and in one piece. Greenland doesn't fly on Sundays and the place was devoid of activity. I turned around and through thick, crunchy snow, walked the couple of miles to town.

Feet freezing, my chest started to wheeze in the crisp air as I slowly wound my way up and down the hills. No one else around. The town was maybe a collection of 50 or so sporadically placed houses painted vivid colours.

The occasional grave was placed along the pathways between the homes and I found that a tad odd. You wouldn't get that in Bolton.

Snow everywhere but there were occasional signs it was thawing out. I knew this because every ten feet or so my feet

Jon Hilton

would disappear beneath me and I'd sink up to my waist. Which becomes a real pisser after a while.

A dozen huskies were chained up away from the housing areas and while I wanted to go stroke them, a sense of self-preservation suggested these were nearly wild animals and probably not used to Brits.

Trudging forward I made my way past a trail of blood in the snow where something had been killed and dragged indoors. I didn't need further reminding that this is a wilderness existence.

Picking out the highest point in the village I half stumbled, half climbed and generally pulled myself up to its' zenith. Looking around in every direction I admired the panorama. Mountains, pristine snow, beautiful skies.

Thirty seconds later I was bored and since there was bugger all to do, I trogged back towards the hotel.

Decision Height

Made my way to my room and lounged around. Bored. Went for my evening meal. Sat next to the window and looked across the wide expanse of snow to the mountains. No choice of food was offered just, 'this is it'. Take it or leave it. I took it. Time dragged.

Back in my room I retrieved my flying paperwork from my smaller rucksack and spread the papers across the spare bed. One of the documents confirmed the aircraft had a Danish connection and I felt better knowing that tomorrow I'd be on my way.

Then checked all the weather data, from my iPad, pulled the curtains closed at 11pm and tried to sleep.

Still daylight outside.

Chapter 8 - Greenland 27th May

Monday

Woke at 5'ish and couldn't quite figure out where I was. Lay awake for two hours pondering the meaning of life whilst just staring at the ceiling.

After breakfast I packed everything into my rucksacks and checked out. The chap at reception mentioned that yesterday's polar bear had wandered too close to a rifle and was now an ex polar bear. Feeling a tad safer I schlepped the 1/2 mile to the airport.

Overcast day.

Decision Height

By 8am I was wandering past various offices in the airport building trying to find the spiral staircase to the Tower. No one stopped me and I poked my head into every office on the ground floor.

The different managers in the offices seemed to be Danish and Greenland's native population appeared to be confined to roles involving heavy lifting.

Finally finding the staircase I wound my way upwards to the Tower and plonked all my belongings on to the settee. The atmosphere seemed a little less cheerful than the Saturday.

Jon Hilton

I said hi and followed that up by saying, *'I've found my paperwork and the aircraft was registered in Denmark'*. The look I got suggested that wouldn't be enough.

Jesper picked up the phone and rang the guys at Nuuk, the nation's capital, to ask about Ultralights / Microlights and their legality in Greenland. The impression I got, as I eaves dropped, was that Nuuk didn't have any position on light aircraft and that made me feel quite cheerful.

Sadly that wasn't sufficient for Jesper. He looked at me, took a long drag on his roll up cigarette, and told me he'd call the Danish CAA to get their perspective. They control the Greenlandic skies and make up the rules.

He called Europe and a conversation took place in Danish. I was perched on the settee biting my finger nails. Jesper hung up and said, *'sorry Jon we can't let you fly anywhere'*. My stomach dropped. The impression I had was that the aircraft was going to be impounded.

I'm a Black belt in Ju-jitsu, 13 stone and 6ft tall, and had visions of a bloody good tussle followed by my flying back to Iceland. Then I thought, 'don't get upset, don't get annoyed, put a smile on your face again and find a way through this'.

My thought process was something along the lines of, 'the chaps in Greenland are working at the far flung dominions of Danish influence and I could be a mechanism for someone to make a name for himself'.

I'm quite good at playing the cheerful, optimistic, twit and the way to go seemed to be to make a polite nuisance of myself in order to resolve matters.

Ten minutes later I'd convinced Jesper that I had reason to speak to the guy in Denmark and he started dialling on my

Decision Height

behalf. He passed over the phone and said the chap was called Henrik.

This new part of the equation started the conversation by saying, *'you have a big problem, my friend'*. And he wouldn't let me get a word in for the next five minutes whilst explaining that Greenland doesn't like Microlights and certainly doesn't want to promote their being flown in the Country.

In return I tried to mount my defence.

I said I'd checked all the AIP guides and none of the airports listed any restrictions. I said I'd seen a picture of the Indian Airforce aircraft, which flew around the world, sat on the same spot where India Zulu was. I mentioned that the Ferry firm I'd spoken to didn't say there was any problem with Microlights and I'd specifically asked the question in writing.

Jokingly I even said a solicitor friend of mine had said Microlights go through Greenland all the time. The Danish chap immediately interrupted me and said, *'they don't'*.

At that point I decided to shut up.

I was trying to make him like me and accepting my medicine seemed like the way to go. It's very rare I lose my temper and when I do it's generally because I feel the need to defend my friends or confront a bully. This chap was just doing his job and he figured me for a trespasser.

Searching for something positive to say I asked, *'what can I do to make things right'*? He replied with a flat, *'you need to make an application for me to consider'*. There was a chink of light in that. I said, *'ok'* and in return he gave me a list of things he wanted to see.

I started jotting down everything he said....

Jon Hilton

The aforementioned items included a letter from the British Civil Aviation Authority saying they both knew of the flight and that I was a competent pilot. My GA flying licence. A written statement saying why I'd entered Danish / Greenlandic airspace without permission.

He wanted the documents covering my Search & Rescue policy. A statement from the firm saying they specifically knew I was in Greenland. Confirmation of an unlimited Search & Rescue budget.

Plus my medical documents. The aircraft's Airworthiness details. My passport. Aircraft Weight and Balance calculations for each leg of the flight. Details of my GPS equipment. Pictures of the aircraft. And a range of additional items for polar survival over and above the kit I had.

As an afterthought, and it seemed he was asking for anything he could think of, he asked for my insurance details for the aircraft.

My initial reaction was, *'oh fuck'*. What I said was, *'ok'*.

Then I said, *'if I get all those items ticked off can I fly on, please?'* He said, *'I'll consider it, but you need to understand this isn't the best start to the process'*.

For good measure he also said there'd be an hourly administration fee to be paid which, as a cheapskate, really, really, pissed me off.

I thanked him for his time and said I'd get back to him as soon as I could with all the details. After saying goodbye I passed the phone back to Jesper.

The overall impression I'd been given was that the Dane's perceive Brits to be 'gung-ho' risk takers who really needed to stay at home and stop being a nuisance.

Decision Height

Sitting back on the settee, I tried to think my way through the problems. I hadn't done a weight and balance calculation for 15 years, it's not relevant on the CT and I had no idea what to do.

The CAA thing would be tricky, very tricky. Buying kit in the town should be easy. The rest I could slowly tick off, I hoped. The major headaches would be the aircraft insurance and Search & Rescue requirements.

I chatted to the two guys in the Tower and started making phone calls from my mobile and checking the Internet. Going online is expensive in Greenland. We take it for granted but it's not the ubiquitous service it is in England.

The weather momentarily cheered up but I could see more clouds and murk rolling in.

A very decent chap called Steve Cooke got involved and started to pull strings. Deepak of London Airsports leapt to my aide. Jesper offered to scan documents for me, which was good of him and I started passing over papers to fax to Henrik.

What I couldn't get was the policy documentation from the Search & Rescue firm in Texas. I had a specific email saying I was covered which then referred me to their website for the terms and conditions. Even though it had a Policy number on it, Jesper said that wouldn't be good enough.

Phoning the company in the States I was told it was a public holiday. Labor Day or Memorial Day or some such and no one could help me. Frustration started to take hold.

Before I knew it the day was over and the airport was closing.

Feeling empty inside, I walked onto the gravel apron and checked the aircraft. She seemed fine.

With a red rucksack hanging from each shoulder I trudged the half mile through the snow back to the hotel.

Checked in again. Which was a damn depressing experience. You feel like you're just haemorrhaging cash.

Chapter 9 - Greenland 28th May

Tuesday

Woke up at 5am and desperately tried to nod off, again. I loathe early mornings. The bed was uncomfortable and the daylight was trying to assault my eyes.

By 7.30am I'd washed, eaten breakfast, checked out and was walking through the snow to the airport. There were huskies chained up along the way and I'd been warned they bit the unwary. The blighters were making disconcerting howling noises.

Jon Hilton

Bob on 8am I was at the base of the Tower. Made it up the spiral stairs with all my kit and resumed my place on the settee. An impressive amount of bright sunlight was bouncing around the inside of the glass structure.

Jesper and the young native chap I'd taken to calling Bob seemed pleased to see me.

Using my mobile I called the SAR (Search & Rescue) firm in Texas. The adviser was very polite but said she couldn't provide a specific statement confirming their geographic coverage and that I wouldn't be able to buy unlimited cover.

For good measure she informed me that their Vice President had taken an extra day's holiday and there were no managers available for me to plead my case too. My blood started to boil.

Whilst speaking to the USA I could tell that even though Jesper and Bob were shuffling paperwork around that they were listening intently to the conversation.

The next phone call was to England in an attempt to sort out a statement from the CAA saying that, despite the evidence, I wasn't a complete dick. I then spent three hours trawling the Internet, on my phone, trying to find unlimited SAR cover.

Then retrieved the aircraft manual from my smaller rucksack and began trying to figure out the bloody weight and balance calculations.

At the same time I put thought into the aircraft insurance details and that anxiety was steadily bubbling away inside me.

Before leaving the UK I'd spoken to two ferry pilots who said that at the point an aircraft landed at a commercial airport the cost of the landing fee covered any ground incidents or accidents. The inference being that I could get by without insuring the aircraft.

Decision Height

The opposing perspective came from a lawyer friend of mine who suggested I'd be responsible for any ground based incident or accident of any description. And I could just imagine the Danes using that as a reason to seize the aircraft.

If India Zulu was blown into an expensive Air Greenland turboprop I'd be paying through the nose for the rest of my natural life... Nothing to be done, though, but stay positive and try to absorb the pressure.

That was how my day was going. Beautiful day. Fluffy clouds. Patches of blue. Impressive mountains. Lots of problems.

I enlisted the help of a Ferry Pilot called Rob and he volunteered to help with the European fella whilst I planned to fight my way through the snow into town.

Possibly because they were too polite to ask me to bugger off, and wait elsewhere for the bad news, the guys in the Tower actively started to help.

Comment was made that one of the ground crew might take me to town by snow mobile, for a price, to pick up the additional survival kit. I'd no idea how it'd fit into the aircraft but I said, *'yep, count me in'* and thirty minutes later found myself astride a snow mobile.

The driver was a young native chap and I was perched behind him. The huskies chained up 20 ft away started to howl. Possibly a matter of professional jealousy. The engine kicked into life and I reached behind and grabbed hold of the brace bars.

81

Jon Hilton

Bloody good fun those things. First time on one. We set off with the engine growling underneath us and raced towards town. Despite holding on for dear life there was a damn big grin on my face as the bracingly cold air rushed at me.

Fifteen minutes later we were in town and through a mixture of broken English, and gesturing, my driver pointed to the only shop. The inference was that he'd come back for me.

Not a big place. Internally it was maybe 30ft long with two aisles. 4 or 5 native folk pottering about. I wandered around the store, both looking gormless and staring at the stock. Everything from big bathroom mirrors to Mars bars.

There was pretty much everything I wanted. Two extra flares, string, large saw, gas stove and they all made it onto the counter. There was still the need for a gas canister and the shop had sold out. Bugger.

The few locals were friendly and smiley but they seemed to be a little uneasy around outsiders. I asked if they had any ideas about the canister and subsequently found an older guy, who in stuttering English, suggested he had one at home he'd sell.

We seemed to enter a bartering process. Good fun, in a way, with lots of smiles and gesturing. I'd no idea whether I was being asked to pay £5 or £50 for the six inch tall canister. We shook on the deal and it turned out his son was the snow mobile driver and he promised my new piece of kit would be delivered to the airport later that day.

Walking outside with my new purchases I was hoping to see my ride. I heard the throaty roar of the snowmobile, as it zipped past me and started to disappear into the distance. Fuck.

It's not really a great day out when you need to walk a couple of miles through snow, some waist deep, with damn big Polar bears on the prowl.

Decision Height

Fortunately my gaze fell upon two western guys stumbling up a hill, a quarter of a mile away. With a mighty effort I caught up to them and tried to strike up a conversation. They'd flown in the previous day in a Cirrus.

I figured the old adage was correct in that if we spotted a polar bear all that was needed was for me to outrun these two. So I decided to stick with them.

One fella was my age and the other was mid-twenties. Worst case I'd pick up a silver medal in the race to safety. Having done the Pamplona Bull Run experience points me to the fact there's very little that can out accelerate me when I'm seriously crapping myself.

The three of us chatted as we stumbled, half sunk in the deeper snow and ice, and generally hiked the three'ish miles homeward.

Seemed like nice fellas. Taking their piece of kit from the Czech Republic to the US. A very sensible IFR aircraft.

We heard a lot of huskies howling, some we saw and some we didn't, and I couldn't make my mind up whether they were being noisy because another predator was looking for a snack or they wanted stroking. An hour or so later me and my human shields made it back to the hotel in 3 regular sized pieces.

My trainers were wet through and jeans were soaked to the waist. What the hell was I doing in this bloody part of the world? I despise the cold.

After a shower, and a period of hand washing all my clothes it was time for tea. The two guys were seated in the restaurant and I spent an hour trying to think up things to chat about, like you do, to keep the conversation flowing.

Jon Hilton

The younger chap was an airline pilot and that gave me sufficient ammunition to wile away the hours.

Later that evening I figured out all my weight and balance calculations for each leg of the journey through Danish Airspace.

Round about midnight I emailed everything over to Denmark from my phone.

Still daylight outside.

Chapter 10 - Greenland 29th May

Wednesday

The same rigmarole happened. Awake at 5am. Tried to sleep on. Couldn't. Ate an early breakfast, checked out, and stumbled through the cold and snow with all my kit strapped to my back. Sun shining.

I climbed the steps to the Tower and plonked my two overly stocked rucksacks on the very familiar settee. Time to tackle the Americans, again.

Jon Hilton

With the time difference an email had already appeared from the British suggesting I was a competent pilot, so that box was now ticked. I looked towards the ceiling and quietly mouthed a *'thank you'* to Deepak and Steve for being such solid guys.

Then checked the weather in the optimistic expectation of a flight south. Lovely day. The sun was making everywhere look beautiful.

For some unfathomable reason I volunteered, don't know why, to clean the Tower windows. My offer was well received but politely declined.

The guys had been really good and they seemed to be sympathising with my plight.

An hour later an email appeared from the Texans confirming the Search & Rescue policy covered Greenland. They wouldn't increase my policy from £50k to an unlimited amount, though.

Decision Height

I tried a dozen SAR insurance firms by email and phone. No one offered unlimited cover. Calling Air Greenland they said they'd need two weeks to assess the risks, which was no bloody use whatsoever.

Thinking laterally I tried to dredge up another solution. Hence in as legalised terminology as I could muster, I wrote an email saying that in the event of a crash I'd fund any additional recovery costs in excess of £50,000. It then went on to say that if any mission was to recover my body, that my Estate via my Will would cover those costs.

I'd be a popsicle by then so I wouldn't care. Having said that I wanted to preserve as much money as possible for my daughter and family. Emailed that to both my Danish CAA contact and my solicitor in England in the hope it'd be good enough.

Humorously, depending upon your mind-set, my Will contained the sum of £10,000 to my dad. He was waiting for a heart op' in the next fortnight but he'd receive the said amount if, in the event of my untimely passing, he bared his bum at the top of the steps leading up to Bolton Town Hall.

If he chose not to, the money would go to charity. As a former insolvency accountant and serious individual there was no way he'd do it but throughout 3 incarnations of my Will the thought of his dilemma has always put a crafty smile on my face.

My ex-girlfriend, the evil genius, had to dive with sharks in South Africa to get her £20,000. It's rare that I feel sorry for sharks but one day they're going to know what it's like to be near a vicious, man eating, predator.

Most folk had a forfeit they had to hurdle, to benefit from my very sad demise. I'm what you might call a mischievous chap.

The last document emailed over was the existing insurance certificate for the aircraft. It included European coverage and

Jon Hilton

listed a few other countries. What it didn't include was the country where I was sat. Nothing I could do. Maybe he wouldn't read it.

Speaking to Rob an hour or two later he seemed quite bullish about my flying onwards. Between him and the Danish fella they seemed to have reached an agreement that I was both a twit but also capable of completing the flight without incident.

Jesper called Henrik, too. They spoke in Danish, and whilst I'd no idea what was being said, if I had to guess I'd say he was batting on my behalf.

After lounging on the settee for another hour an email arrived saying permission to fly on had been granted with the proviso that I abide by Cap BL9-6 and that my whole trip was beyond Danish Airspace by the 9th June. I readily agreed. 11 days should be plenty.

With an ironic smile on his face Jesper read out the conditions of Cap BL9-6. That meant no flying above 10,000ft and ruled out the shortest route over the icecap towards the west coast. It'd add at least 4 days onto the trip but I readily agreed. No choice.

It also meant the additional kit purchased from the store was no longer required and that felt a tad frustrating. Sensible to have onboard, mind.

For the sake of reference it seems a lot of guys fly above 10,000ft without oxygen. I'd always worried about hypoxia, a lack of oxygen to the brain, and had that pinned to the front of my mental chalkboard. According to more seasoned pilots it's doable for certain stints.

At the same time I'd already had a shed load of anxieties about potentially flying above the icecap. The need to be above 12,000ft isn't something Samson enjoys, and neither do I.

Decision Height

Plus the scare stories had made an impression. Hypoxia and crashing. Losing sight of the horizon and crashing. Experiencing a complete white out and crashing. Hence flying the long way round the coast carried a certain appeal.

I resisted the temptation to say that Cap BL9-6 was written on the assumption that Microlights only burn 'car fuel'. And that's why it's not suitable for flying at altitudes above 6,000. ie. in case there's a vapour lock and the engine stops.

Samson was fuelled with the Avgas we'd picked up at Kulusuk so flying above the ice cap wouldn't be a problem. Having said that sometimes you just can't battle bureaucracy.

With all the boxes now ticked I picked my stuff up feeling damn pleased to be on my way. Then started to feel scared again. And then Jesper looked at me through the fumes of his hand rolled cigarette and said I wouldn't make it to Narsass before they closed. Fucking typical.

Ten minutes later, approximately 1.30pm local time, I was checking the aircraft. There were a couple of specks of antifreeze on the nose wheel spat. I really hate it when she leaks.

With cold fingers I removed the engine cowling and had a good nosey. Very tentatively, like there were explosives attached to the engine, I prodded different bits hoping to god nothing moved more than it should.

Still plenty in the antifreeze reservoir. No obvious leaks. A few specks shouldn't be a killer, should it? That'd happened a few times in the UK over the last year or two but it plays on your mind... Would it just be a slow drip or would it become a catastrophic failure at some point?

Jon Hilton

I tried further tightening 3 rubber hoses attaching themselves to the engine by adding more cable ties, and then reattached the cowling.

Walking away from the aircraft my snowmobile friend appeared. In stuttering English he apologised for leaving me behind the previous day. Apparently someone had fallen through the ice and needed rescuing.

Decision Height

I didn't ask whether the person had survived on the basis I'd really rather not know.

Made my way back to the hotel and after 10 minutes of forlornly ringing the reception bell someone appeared and checked me in, again.

With cleanliness being next to godliness an hour passed whilst all my 'red' thermal shirts, socks and undies got a hand wash.

As an aside, I saw the original Star Trek series as a kid. On any visit to an alien planet it's always the bugger in the red shirt that dies first. That thought made me both smile and shake my head.

Chapter 11 - Greenland 30th May

Thursday

Rudely awakened at 6am as two text messages arrived from England. Still it was a comparative lie in compared to recent days. I cursed and tried to sleep on, without any success.

I'd checked the weather yesterday and was feeling nervous. I expected a little unpleasantness on the flight south but it would hopefully cheer up further along the coast. That was no great consolation. Everything was playing on my mind.

Decision Height

Me and my bags checked out of the hotel and made our way to the airport. I started to say my goodbyes and the two Tower guys, Jesper and Bob, both shook my hand. In a slightly surreal moment Jesper said they'd miss me.

We'd spent 3 days in the Tower together and, with a touch of Stockholm syndrome kicking in, I'd come to like both fellas. His comment was bizarrely touching.

Jesper called up the weather station on my behalf to check my route south. The lady on the phone suggested I'd be fine following the coast. I asked Jesper his thoughts and he just shrugged.

Conscious of how quickly things seem to change in the North Atlantic the realisation dawned that this lady's opinions could lead to my death. She wasn't familiar with my aircraft or VFR kit in general. The whole thought process was nearly enough to put me off my Kit Kat Chunky.

Jesper mentioned the direct route across the Icecap, which was my original plan, and asked whether I was going that way. After a moment of confusion I said, *'I thought you didn't want me to go in that direction'*. He said he couldn't insist on which way I went if it was for safety reasons.

Then he gave me a 'look' that suggested that route would be simpler, quicker and safer.

I had a vision all this was forming some kind of integrity test and my being clamped in irons if I got the answer wrong. I said I'd follow the coast south to Narsass as agreed with the Danish CAA guy and he nodded in return.

By 10 am I was both incredibly anxious and backtracking the gravel runway to spin through 180 degrees and take off. It'd hopefully take me three and a half hours if the gods were kind.

Jon Hilton

Clearing Kulusuk we flew over the tiny town and headed along the coast. Strapped into the aircraft I looked around the cabin and couldn't help but stare at the SPOT emergency beacon, with it's little LED light flashing on and off. Hopefully it wouldn't be needed.

The cloud base was 1,000ft but then it started to come down. My anxiety was the freezing cloud layer. Clip the icy moist air and there'd be all sorts of headaches.

Flying off the coastline, there was a ridge of cloud on my right, small chunks of ice in the sea, and hazy mist above me. To stay clear of the freezing cloud I found myself at 100ft give or take. The view of the icebergs was bloody impressive but the chilling thought dawned that any lapse in concentration meant total fucking disaster.

Trying to put all complicated thoughts from my mind the plan was simply to fly straight and level. The aircraft was working well and I told myself all I needed to do was focus and jink around anything lumpy. Iceberg or Island.

Decision Height

Yet each minute felt like borrowed time and I felt so incredibly tired, tortured, isolated and numb.

If the engine stuttered, and lost power, I'd be dead within a couple of minutes. That thought drains a person's spirits and the only thing to do was to put my mind into neutral and reach for another Mars bar in the hopeful expectation of a sugar rush.

The low cloud slowly moved away and Samson and I were able to climb to 5,000ft. The view bordered on the spectacular. Mountain peaks. Pristine snow. Sunshine. All very attractive but the question was, 'what the hell am I doing here'?

My plan had been to route direct and cut out a proportion of the southern tip of Greenland by going inland, but I had an attack of the heebie-jeebies. If anything went wrong over the mountains there was zero chance of a survivable landing.

Jon Hilton

Decision Height

Thinking, hoping and second guessing that it was the right thing to do I deviated from my flight plan and followed the coast. At least ditching in the sea would offer a glimmer of hope.

I'd been out of radio contact for hours and wasn't able to tell anyone of my change of plan. On my right the view was stunning with snow 10,000ft above sea level forming a blanket on the horizon.

The mountains flattened out and I had another change of heart, then checked my balls were where they were supposed to be, and cut inland. Found myself continuously listening to the heart beat of the engine and hoping for the best, as we sped along at 100 mph.

I figuratively held my breath for an hour. And took the view I was dead already. Best to think I was a gonner and then the pressure would go away.

It's a very strange process both fearing death whilst also considering how you want to die.

Jon Hilton

The conclusion I came to was that I'd rather pop off after a successful crash landing, in terms of being able to walk away from it, and then die of hypothermia.

The idea of smacking into a jagged mountain peak and having bits of me splatter all over the place seemed very untidy.

I felt my right hand squeezing and releasing something. The CT has two seats that have adjustable lumbar supports. There's a little pneumatic ball that you squeeze to inflate the back of the seat and my train of thought had led me to using it as a stress ball. Try not to die Johnny Boy, for Ava's sake.

With a little misty cloud beneath me Samson navigated her way to the fjords leading to Narsass. Descending into the water filled valleys I called the Tower 20 miles out. No joy.

At 10 miles there was intermittent radio contact. I keyed the mike and could hear a faint, broken voice, trying to reply.

Nothing to do but guess the runway in use and proceed warily. Clear skies but it seemed windy. My airspeed indicator was still kaput but the ground speed readings on the GPS were giving me a few hints about the winds.

Knowing the airspeed I should be doing and with a little deduction my reasoning suggested there was 20 knots or so hitting the aircraft. Potentially unhealthy.

At 5 miles out the radio reception was much better and I confirmed the altimeter setting, runway and winds with the Tower guys. No great problems except instead of landing from the water side of the fjord I needed to fly inland then turn through 180 degrees and come back the way I'd came.

All do-able but after flying for nearly 5 hours and being anxious for the same bloody period it wasn't the straight in landing I'd hoped for. The worry was turbulent air flipping me over as it

Decision Height

cascaded over the hills. Plus Narsass has a reputation for the wind blowing from both ends of the runway and meeting in the middle.

Add in the fact my bladder needed emptying and the day held the prospect of ending messily.

Flying down the valley felt wrong, too close to the hill sides, I turned left base, pulled the throttle back and started to descend. The Dynon began flashing to let me know the engine was cooling too quickly. I reluctantly pushed the throttle forward to keep her warm.

Sun shining, fluffy clouds about, but oppressively cold just outside my little cocoon. Keeping the power on, to prevent the engine from going on strike, India Zulu descended onto final approach. Going too fast.

I side slipped her to lose height. One wing low, with opposite rudder kicked in. Flying her 'out of balance' felt wrong. Felt like I was hurting her. My recurrent, *'o fuck'* feeling, surfaced and I hastily retightened my harness straps.

She floated along the runway and finally settled to earth. We'd taken twice the distance I normally take to land, a good 600m's or so. The airport's big enough for that with 1,800m's of Tarmac to play with. No great drama.

After 4 hours 55 minutes of flying we rolled off the active runway and parked.

Ten minutes later Samson was being refuelled by the ground crew. Shortly after that I was cleaning excess fuel off the wings and really wishing that every bastard that spilled fuel on my wings would have a cricket bat shoved up his arse for at least an hour.

Unsurprisingly I didn't say anything, simply smiled, mopped up the fuel with my sponge and put it in the cabin. There'd be a low level fuel smell for the onward leg courtesy of my refuelling comrades.

After working my way through the airport offices I found the folk I needed and introduced myself.

Sorted things out, checked the next days' weather, and was pointed to the one and only hotel. Very much fatigued and jaded by the days experiences.

Narsass (proper name Narsarsuaq). Population 150. Has a pub that only opens on Saturdays.

Chapter 12 - Greenland, Canada 31st May

Friday

My accommodation was originally built to house US Air Force personnel who'd been stationed in Greenland until 1958. It was then turned over to the Danish authorities who'd taken the military barracks and converted them into a functional, very bland, hotel.

I woke up in a small room at 5.30am, depressed and demoralised. Why the bloody hell hoteliers didn't invest in blackout curtains I had no idea.

Jon Hilton

To add insult to injury, the double glazed unit wouldn't completely seal and there was a draught working its way round the room.

I showered, had some dried meats for breakfast, and made my way the three hundred yards to the Airport building.

Took the normal approach of wandering into each office trying to figure out where the stairs to the Tower were. None of the handful of chaps on duty stopped or questioned me so I carried on nosying around.

After discovering, amongst other rooms, the cleaning cupboard, the final door opened into a stair case and I worked my way upstairs.

There was a reasonably large office with a big map table and two desks at the far end of the rectangular room. On two walls were hosts of business cards pinned to the surface that'd been left by various folk transiting through Narsass.

Decision Height

Two native guys were sat down and they cheerfully said, 'hi'.

I explained who I was and asked for whatever weather charts they could rustle up for the days' flight. I also asked for the telephone number of the weather station in Sondrestome.

The hope was for a little banter with the guys, to get them onside, and noticed one of them had a screensaver on his PC that had a few semi naked ladies on show. Each female flashing by represented a country and my love of blighty led me to say Miss Great Britain was by far the most attractive.

Not the case but patriotism dictated I stand in defence of my little island.

The other guy seemed intrigued and came round to our side of the desk. He took a gander and expressed his support for an American lady. I immediately told him he was both blind and had no right being heterosexual, which got both chaps laughing.

I was trying to be light hearted but felt thoroughly drained and on edge.

Having said that I wanted their thoughts on my flight north. And not just a passive, 'you'll be fine, now go away' but more of a, 'we like you Jon, and we'll keep you safe'.

All three of us looked through the weather charts and they let me call the weather station from their phone. Everything seemed good despite higher winds than I would have liked.

In conjunction with the thoughts of my two friends and the lady on the phone, I made the 'go decision' and asked for a flight plan and pen. The younger of the two guys, who were both around thirty, handed me a biro.

Still feeling a bit twitchy I clicked the pen to get the nib to engage and felt a sharp tingling sensation. Then thought to myself, 'Jonathan you are a complete and utter dick. Get a grip and stop worrying about everything. Your senses are way too bloody heightened'.

I looked up and noticed both guys were grinning at me as I stood there running through my own private diagnostic. Then realised the funny bastards had given me a joke shop pen which'd delivered an electric shock. Smart fucking arses.

Thirty minutes later I was airborne and whizzing down one of the Fjords. Nearly at the coast I took a right turn and began flying north along the shoreline to the country's capital, Nuuk.

Stunning scenery. Amazing colours. Pristine white snow on the horizon to my right. Immaculate mountains. Vivid blues defining the sea and the sky.

I was feeling twitchy but that'd become a permanent state of affairs. At the same time it was becoming easier to see beauty in my surroundings and be awed by the majesty of it.

Decision Height

After three hours Nuuk was in sight. The Air Traffic gent seemed very friendly and gave me a direct approach to the runway only

Jon Hilton

asking that I call 'long final' when established in my descent to land.

Still no airspeed readings courtesy of frozen water in the pitot system. Subconsciously closed the throttle and slowed. Went from minus 15 degree flaps, to zero, to plus 15 degrees and finally put down 30 degrees of flaps.

At each stage my ears were listening to the whine of the flap motors as they forced the aircraft to slow. If I was too fast the flaps would struggle to extend.

Keeping my right hand glued to the throttle I tried to gauge my airspeed and avoid tumbling from the sky.

Decision Height

Running through my landing checks everything seemed fine. The engine instruments were green and I watched as the grey smear of the runway got closer.

India Zulu crossed the runway threshold, at about a 100ft above the asphalt, and hit a vicious updraft of air. One second we were in a gentle descent, everything nice and bonny, the next I was thrown upwards and then immediately slammed down. Fuck.

I felt my weight shifting against the harness as gravity said hello and lobbed me around. I rammed the throttle forward, engine roaring, and desperately tried to cushion the impact against the runway.

My seatbelt had been forced loose, damn poor design, and I had a momentary dilemma of, do I tighten it or just fly the bloody aircraft? I tried to stay calm as time seemed to slow to a stop.

The aircraft was nose up and my first fear was that we'd stall. My second was that we'd crash. She was going straight down like a lift, and the downdraft had full hold.

Full power was helping slow the downward trajectory, but not enough. I forced the stick forward and aimed for the ground in a counter intuitive attempt to build airspeed and continue flying. Please god let this work.

A second passed, and then another. Nerves tingling.

And then time caught up with us and she started to gain airspeed. I tentatively pulled the stick back, to avoid hitting the deck, and we very slowly inched away from the prospective point of impact.

Fifty feet further into the runway and half a dozen feet high I feathered the power, gently pitched back, and we settled to earth. Hell of a roller coaster ride and another cat's life expired.

Jon Hilton

We turned off the active runway and taxied to the apron.

Feeling like I'd been electrocuted I carried out my magneto check, stopped the propeller and switched off all the instruments. Then pulled the Master and finally took the key out of the ignition. My head flopped forward.

Sitting there feeling very fatigued I was reasonably cheerful not to have panicked or broken anything.

Then started to second guess myself. Should I have gone with 15 degrees of flaps and come in faster. Would I have cut through the conditions without the drama or would that have just made matters worse?

She's a Microlight, so when it comes to nasty air I'm in the lap of the gods. There'd been no warning from the Tower about aircraft killing conditions but then again they're not used to the needs of light aircraft.

The flight had been three hours of low level arse twitching topped off with a final 20 seconds of near diarrhoea. The bloody joys of flying.

Got out and stretched. My ears felt numb and I slapped them a couple of times to bring back normality. Disengaged myself from the lower half of my immersion suit and stood up straight, taking in the view.

The refuelling wagon drove over and I filled up with Avgas, again.

The continued use of Aviation fuel was starting to pray on my mind. It has too much lead in it and is like cholesterol to the rest of us. ie. too much equals clogged arteries and a potential seizure.

Decision Height

Then I started to wonder what bureaucracy the nation's capital might have in store. That thought drained me a little as the earlier adrenalin dissipated and the reality of my situation came back to say hello. Approximately 1.30pm local time.

Nothing to do but be cheerful and put my dogged head on. I'm British, don't ya know, and proud to be so. That always gives me an extra level of self confidence.

Slowly walking across the large parking area towards the Tower I had a momentary 'oh fuck' feeling. Nuuk might only be 5% of the size of my home town but, as the nation's capital, that generates a certain mind set from some folk.

Jon Hilton

Inside the building I gate crashed various offices by mistake before being pointed to a counter where I was expected to pay for my landing and fuel.

The lady was very polite and I handed over Mr Mastercard. I pointedly refused to look at the credit card receipt on the basis it'd only upset me knowing how much I was being charged.

Sliding the paperwork into my file of documents I was directed to another door which was the gateway to the Tower. I climbed the ubiquitous spiral staircase and plonked the lighter of my two rucksacks on the settee.

The chaps on duty were both Danish and instantly friendly. I was waiting for someone to ask the weight of the aircraft, as it sat alone on the apron, looking very small. No questions came and they just wanted to chat about life in England.

I told them of my onward destination and asked for weather information. They both provided it and let me use their phone to call the Met Office.

A piece of paper was handed to me and it seemed that Rob, in England, had already filed a flight plan for my onward leg to Iqaluit.

It went without saying that I was tired. The lack of sleep was catching up with me and I didn't want to fly on. I felt like a zombie.

And like a dead man walking, I found myself saying and doing the things I needed to do, but there was no conviction about my actions. Just going through the motions.

I reluctantly called the Canadians Customs people to confirm my onward flight.

Nuuk to Iqaluit

An hour and a half later I was airborne, heading west. By many standards it was a lovely day.

The difference in weather over the course of 500 miles can be treacherous. Life and death. Flying by VFR rules go out the window in favour of staying alive.

Jon Hilton

I managed to keep in radio contact with Nuuk Tower, and then the Greenland Approach frequency, until the International boundary.

Passed over my latitudes and longitudes and said my goodbyes with the hope of immediately picking up the Air Traffic support offered by Quebec Centre and the Canadians.

The Canadians weren't responding when I called. No answer, just static.

That triggered a specific moment where I thought, 'you've done it fella, made it to Canadian airspace, just turn round and head back'. I didn't, but my levels of mental exhaustion and anxiety were increasing.

I was at 5,000ft, feeling chilly. At least if the engine failed I'd have time to fully get the immersion suit on. I couldn't imagine anyone being sent to rescue me 'till after I'd died but, ho hum.

The cloud layer underneath me thickened up and looked like densely matted cotton wool. No way through and it seemed to extend far beyond the horizon. If I needed to descend through it there'd be a problem.

With only a percentage of my brain working I figured it'd be wise to turn back and find a break in the cloud. Then fly within sight of the sea.

Iqaluit was reportedly overcast and I'd used up all my blind luck so far hence the plan was to backtrack and descend. That would mean wasting more fuel by retreating but better to make a planned withdrawal and then turn back en route when possible.

Decision Height

The nightmare scenario was getting blocked by walls of cloud and having to do any number of about turns. Worst case I'd run out of fuel and splash into the freezing ocean.

I dipped a wing, kicked the rudder, and spun through 180 degrees. After 10 minutes of pointing in the wrong direction I spotted the sea, dived, levelled out and turned back on track.

Firmly inside Canadian airspace I called again, to no avail. Made a series of calls but couldn't raise anyone. More brain numbing patience required.

For an agonising 2 and a half hours I was without radio contact. I kept trying to make relay transmissions to other aircraft, without success. It's soul destroying making calls no one answers.

Jon Hilton

'Quebec Centre this is Golf Charlie Golf India Zulu come in please'.

And then when no reply came I started making blind calls in the hope that whilst I couldn't hear anyone maybe they could hear me.

'Quebec Centre, Golf Charlie Golf India Zulu enroute from Nuuk to Iqaluit. Currently at 63 degrees 31 minutes North and 58 degrees 27 minutes West request basic service'.

After the fourth attempt I gave up and started trying different radio frequencies to see if anyone was around. No joy. I was on my own again and that bites.

The better weather in Greenland retreated behind me. I could feel the warmth leaving the cockpit and looked out to see a bank of cloud in front of me. Knowing Iqaluit was overcast if I went over the cloud, I might not be able to descend through it without icing and eventual mortality issues.

Another life and death decision required. Under or over? More of an involuntary act than a conscious decision, I pushed the throttle forward, pulled the stick back and climbed. It felt colder inside the cabin. The Airspeed Indicator readings on the Dynon started to read hundreds of miles per hour. The same instrument was suggesting a 99 knot head wind.

Neither reading could be right. Or could they? Was I supposed to extrapolate some form of hypothesis? Would the wings come off?

So bloody drained by all the thinking and second guessing I just resigned myself to dying. That's the only way to get through moments of potential panic. Just say, 'fuck off world, I'm not going to be intimidated. I'll just do my best and see what happens'.

Decision Height

The outside air temperature was showing at minus 10c. I'd always thought it under read by 5c or so. Was it really minus 15c or even minus 20c?

Seeing a small break in the cloud Samson descended. Not as if I'd lose contact with anyone. It felt like playing a video game at this point.

Below the cloud I could see small chunks of ice, like ice cubes in a damn big glass. From 500ft above, the sea looked incredibly blue. Nearing the Canadian coast I kept calling on the radio but no one was listening. Too low.

The ice started to thicken and it felt much more oppressive. The mountains looked unfriendly. There were moments where I caught sight of blue skies and then minutes of completely obscured sky. Scared and feeling alone my focus switched to the throb of the engine.

Jon Hilton

Then started to question the type of person I am. Why would I take any risks in general? Am I a hopeless thrill seeker? Was the Danish guy correct to subtly suggest Brits are a lost cause?

My gaze caught the entrance to Frobisher Bay from about 30 miles out and it didn't look a very attractive sight. Mountains on either side, with cloud obscuring the tops, meant I couldn't take the shorter route across the headland.

Subsequently spent an hour flying up the bay towards the airport. Small mountains, if there is such a term, on either side.

The bay itself is mostly frozen over with pockets of water visible. Maybe 150 miles long and 20 plus miles wide. It looked desolate and unwelcoming. If the engine failed there was a chance of a successful landing on the ice, but I'd perish there.

Occasionally the clouds thinned and I could see blue above me.

Decision Height

Getting nearer to the airport I tried again to make radio contact with Quebec Centre, and failed. At 15 miles out Samson was at 1,000ft bumping along underneath the cloud base, and I managed to make contact with Iqaluit Tower.

Rehearsing what I was going to say I tried to sound professional as I introduced myself and gave my position report. The fella confirmed the runway, winds, and the pressure settings in the American format.

That threw me. I wrote down everything he said and then repeated it back verbatim. He seemed happy.

I'd been expecting the pressure settings in Pascal's and he'd given them in Inches of Mercury. I knew the system was different in Canada but that piece of information had been filed somewhere in the back of my mind.

Twigging the change in pressure units I leant forward to adjust the Dynon and change the settings from the equivalent of Metric to Imperial. Then thought, 'sod it, I'm not mentally up for that' and leaned back in my seat deciding I'd just guess my heights, and try not to fuck up the landing.

The Airspeed Indicator wasn't working so it'd be a case of guesswork all round.

Five miles out two commercial jets came on frequency and it seemed they'd arrive at the same time as myself and India Zulu. Great, just what I needed. Fuck, cock, bollocks.

The Air Traffic guy seemed happy for me to land first, but I wasn't. Didn't want to feel rushed. Didn't want to get in the way. I volunteered to let both of them go in first.

The Air Traffic chap broadcast that the, *'Microlight traffic will extend to stay clear'*.

Jon Hilton

Increasing my downwind and base legs I spotted the two 737's appear through the gloom. One after the other they cancelled their IFR approach having visually picked up the dark smear of the runway.

I got no comment or thanks for patiently waiting for the two passenger jets. Sitting there, freezing my tits off, any kind of pleasantry would have been nice.

After watching the commercial aircraft land I lined up on final approach and began slowing India Zulu. Then started looking around outside the aircraft.

There was a damned pretty river meandering its way in front of the runway. The powdery blue colour suggested water beneath an icy surface. Everything screamed, 'cold'.

The yellow coloured terminal building was just visible on my right.

Decision Height

All things insurance were playing on my mind but the only attitude I felt able to take was to say 'fuck it'. The thought occurred to me that I should get the phrase tattooed across my forehead, but instantly decided that'd look silly.

Trying to stay above the glide path of the jets, and with fingers crossed, I pulled the throttle back and floated her beyond the point where both 737's had landed.

Samson was too high and too fast but we were descending. After what seemed like an age we gently settled to earth. I felt a little 'give' in one of the tyres as the wheels met the Tarmac. Something not quite right.

Slowing to a walking pace I taxied off the active runway and with the directions of the Air Traffic Controller ringing in my

Jon Hilton

ears parked near the Avgas fuel drums. Shutting down the engine I unclipped the harnesses and put my head in my hands.

Still alive Johnny Boy.

Peeling myself from the cockpit my feet touched Canadian ground. With my immersion suit half on and half off I slowly stood up, stretched, and tried to get the throbbing noise out of my head by repeatedly slapping my ears.

I felt better. Mission accomplished. Then realised I was only halfway through the trip. Somewhere thousands of miles away was the bustling metropolis of Bolton. Centre of the universe.

The refuelling chap appeared. India Zulu needed about 85 litres but the miserable bugger said I'd have to buy the whole drum,

Decision Height

every drop. I'd known that but had hoped there'd be some flexibility. There wasn't.

Being a cheapskate, even a tired one, I couldn't help but worry I'd be buying much more than needed. It seemed like such a bloody waste.

No doubt someone was going to get 120 litres of Avgas for free. Nearly $200 of my hard earned cash would be going to waste. Bugger.

There was a moment where I'd thought about asking for Mogas to be put in the aircraft, but I was simply too drained to even contemplate asking for anything complicated.

A large SUV slowly drove up to Samson and Agent Godspell and his colleague from customs climbed out. Both big fellas with sunglasses on. It was cold, round about freezing, and they wanted to check over the aircraft. I said hi and that it was completely fine for them to rummage around.

They asked about my reason for being in Canada. I said a 10 hour stay. That completely threw them. I volunteered to take everything out of the aircraft for inspection. In return I got the all too familiar look that said, 'you're an idiot' and was simply asked to show my passport.

Twenty minutes later I was in a tiny Portacabin with two Canadians trying to remember my PIN code to pay for the fuel. 8 or 9 o'clock by then. I got the number right but the card was declined. Fuck.

Seemingly MasterCard get confused when you cross continents. They suspect fraud and cancel everything. Which is a real pisser. Payment was finally made with another card and an apology.

An hour later I'd introduced myself to the FBO gents and subsequently pulled Samson by hand onto a small piece of

Jon Hilton

gravel by the side of their building. There was nothing to tie her down to and there was no way I was leaving her to be blown away during the night.

Looking around my frigidly cold surroundings I spotted four heavy wooden railway sleepers about 30ft away. Asking one of the guys to help me we heaved them towards the aircraft.

Positioning two underneath each wing I got out my tie down kit, attached the eyelets to each wing, and with freezing fingers managed to lash the rope around each sleeper. Very tired. Bone achingly cold.

With her hopefully secured for the night I spoke to the FBO manager, arranged for collection the next morning and was driven to a small hotel. Then checked in and was given the tiniest room in the world.

Late evening by then and I needed to fill my empty stomach. Braving the frigid cold I walked from the hotel to a cheap local restaurant. Low ceilings and a collection of sad faced locals greeted me. The residents were all eating competitively priced items and I had some form of unappetising Chinese meal.

Thirty minutes later I proceeded to leave. On the way out I saw a sign on the notice board which would have seemed out of place in my home town. It read, **'Warning, Syphilis is on the rise in Nunavut'**. I looked around and couldn't understand why.

Walking back from the diner I spotted a convenience store and bought a few trinkets for the family back home. Baseball hats & beef jerky for dad.

I didn't think he'd know what it was but it'd be fun watching him try it.

By 11pm I was asleep.

Decision Height

Jon Hilton

Chapter 13 - Canada, Greenland 1st June

Saturday

The alarm went off at 4am, local time, which is never a good start to any day. I struggled to open my eyes and for the umpteenth time reluctantly got out of bed. Drew the curtains and looked out the hotel window.

Not the best of views. Not a prosperous place. From what I could tell Iqaluit is just a stopping off point for folk going elsewhere.

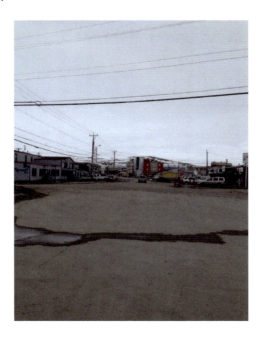

Decision Height

It's not a centre for tourism. Between the Nunavut province of Canada and Greenland they have the two highest suicide rates in the world.

I made it to the hotel reception where the FBO gent was waiting to drive me to the airport. Not for the first time I questioned my sanity. And then his for volunteering to pick me up at such an ungodly hour.

Pleasant chap. He explained how he liked the warm weather and that at this point of the year it was usually warmer. A story I'd heard quite a bit.

We drove through the security checkpoint at the airport. The lady on duty looked miserable and I completely sympathised. My need was to get out of Canada as soon as humanly possible.

The FBO office is a single storey affair. Large reception area with settees in the centre and a couple of computers set against the wall. Gravitating towards the machines I began exploring the available weather information, trying to merge the Canadian and Greenland data.

Rob, in the UK, thought it was a no go for today due to high winds and freezing fog. I went through my routine of checking the sources I knew and then looking for other slivers of local information in the hope of flying.

Telling my FBO friend that the weather forecast didn't look good for at least a couple of hours I said I'd go outside and prep the aircraft in the hope of a later flight. 7am by then.

Opening the door to the outside world was a mistake. Overcast and bitingly cold. Clad in hat and gloves I walked to India Zulu and began untying her from the log sleepers she'd been secured to. The hat was itchy and the gloves weren't helping with the knots so I took them all off, and felt even more miserable.

125

Jon Hilton

Grabbing hold of two bitterly cold propeller blades I heaved the aircraft from the gravel area and slowly pulled her onto the tarmac.

With my fingers freezing and ears going numb I began my pre-flight inspection of India Zulu. The thought went through my mind that Samson would die in this climate if she had to sit here for days waiting for the weather to improve.

I opened the engine access hatch and checked the oil levels. They looked a little lower than the previous day. Still good to go, though.

Depressingly the left tyre looked down. Not completely flat, but not fully inflated. I wrapped my fingers around the composite prop', touching the frigid material again, and pulled her forward a few feet. The condition of the tyre looked slightly better.

Minus 5c at that point. It would be bloody uncomfortable changing the tyre and my fingers simply weren't up to the task. The tyre might survive another landing, if it survived the taxiing process.

A very tired voice in the back of my mind was telling me an accident on touchdown would be expensive and without insurance I was risking the aircraft, again.

Hands in pockets I walked up the stairs to the FBO office and mentally decided, despite all logic, to go in an hours' time.

I sat on the settee in the office, tilted my head backwards, and tried to sleep. Didn't manage to nod off but felt better for having closed my eyes. So drained. So stressed. So tired of it all.

The weather forecast didn't look particularly attractive. Nuuk was overcast with freezing fog. An aircraft killer. There was a weather front in the way. An airport further into Greenland looked possible but it'd mean testing the range of the aircraft.

Decision Height

Decision made. Today was the day to die. Might happen. Might not. A fifty, fifty call. I was seeing the world through a haze, but I was leaving Canada.

I paid my fees and had the chap take a picture of me by the aircraft. Said my goodbyes and reluctantly began putting on my immersion suit, or at least the lower half of it. Then climbed into the aircraft and took a moment to pause and ponder.

Put the key in the ignition, shouted, *'clear prop'* and turned the key. The starter motor clicked into life, the propeller rotated four times and then stopped.

Too cold.

Jon Hilton

Tried to start the engine again. The prop' span three times and stopped. There was a horrible whirring noise. Not good.

I kept the choke on but completely closed the throttle. Tried again and she reluctantly fired into life. I knew then she wouldn't survive if we stayed in Iqaluit any longer.

Ten or so hours in Canada seemed long enough.

With the prop' spinning I warmed the engine up to temperature, radioed the Tower for taxi instructions and started to move. The tyre felt ok but I could tell it wasn't fully inflated. The cabin started to warm up a little. Five minutes later we were airborne.

Flying down Frobisher Bay the aim was to fly at 1,500ft but courtesy of the overcast skies the highest I could manage was 1,000ft. Miserable, grey, cold day. The heater was on full but it was bone chillingly cold in the cabin.

The bay looked unwelcoming. A hundred and fifty miles of nowhere to land. Mostly frozen over. I flew on because I was too stupid to turn back and too tired to put more thought into the flight.

There was a hollow feeling in the pit of my stomach that only a Kit Kat Chunky could cure.

Decision Height

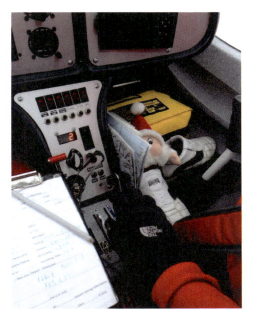

Jon Hilton

I felt a little better as we coasted out but by that point there'd been no radio contact for 100 or so miles and none of the frequencies I'd been given had resulted in contact with anyone. I was alone again and it was grinding away at me.

The sky started to open, the clouds retreated, and there was an opportunity to climb. My paperwork was for a VFR clearance at 5,000 ft but figuring height would equal radio reception I gently pushed the throttle forward, pulled the stick back and started to ascend. After an eternity I topped out at 7,000ft and spent an hour floating above a sea of white.

Still couldn't raise anyone on the radio and with more cloud appearing above Samson I couldn't fly any higher. With overcast gloom above and scattered cloud beneath me we were the meat in a very chilly sandwich.

If the layers of cloud didn't squeeze and engulf the aircraft, which would be a killer, the headache was where to land in Greenland.

Mentally I was on auto pilot by then and figured unless the weather improved I was buggered.

A hole appeared and I dived straight through it. Levelling out at 700ft, I could see small chunks of ice floating on the sea. The odd cloud got in the way of the view and we jinked around them whilst trying to stay on track towards Greenland.

Everything looked dangerous. Clipping a cloud would mean ice on the wings and possibly a disastrous splash in the sea. Without radio contact with a responsible adult I'd be dead long before anyone got to me and my organ donor card would be bloody useless.

Decision Height

Beneath the covering of cloud it started to drizzle. Hitting the aircraft and instantly crystallising into ice on both the wings and windscreen. Fuck.

Instant decision. No time to think. I rammed the stick forward and dived. Felt light headed. Put her into an 80 degree banked turn, with the left wing pointing at the sea and the right towards heaven.

India Zulu flattened out of dive 50ft above the dark blue sea. I felt the G-force throughout my body and realised there was a lot more blood in my feet than there should be.

Pulled the stick back and shot upwards. I was dodging cloud, banking left and right, but we were clear of the rain and climbing as we fled.

Jon Hilton

Samson started to slow but we were gaining altitude with every intimidating second. I found a tiny break in the misty cloud and squeezed through into bright sunlight.

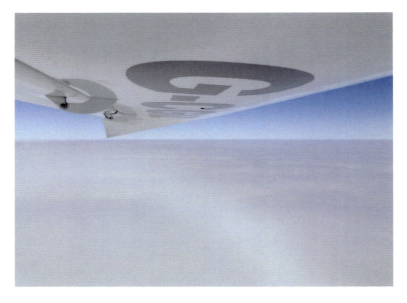

At 5,000ft I turned back onto my heading. My head was swivelling left and right every couple of minutes checking out the condition of the wings. It was showing a chilly minus 9c on the Dynon but for the next 20 minutes the ice started to retreat from the surface of the aircraft as the sun attacked it.

The ubiquitous moggy had just lost life number five.

I began making blind radio calls but no one was answering. Above the cloud there was still the dilemma of where to land. I didn't want to go to the destination on my flight plan. That seemed too far away for my concentration levels to remain useful. I made a subconscious decision to divert to Nuuk.

By that point I was midway between Canada and Greenland and still couldn't reach anyone on the radio. I'd already had to

Decision Height

deviate from my flight plan and any rescue team would be looking in the wrong location.

Realising I was slipping away mentally I found my caffeine tablets. Didn't take any but kept rustling the metal blister pack between my fingers.

I'd gone through every frequency on my Garmin but hadn't been able to make contact with anyone. With my right hand I got out all my paperwork, including all the weather printouts, and with one hand on the stick started to leaf through everything looking for other frequencies.

It was difficult to read, fly and make notes without losing height or affecting my track. My flying was all over the place. Gaining height, losing height, going off course.

I ran out of space on my kneepad to write down possible radio frequencies so I started scribbling on anything.

Courtesy of the fact my bare feet were in the immersion suit, my trainers were handy and I jotted possible frequencies on the blighters. Then starting making blind calls across half a dozen of them.

Jon Hilton

'Golf Charlie Golf India Zulu to anyone on frequency come in please'. No response. Time and again I tried.

My pressure levels were escalating. My head felt like it was stuffed with cotton wool. But at the same time I was resigned to the day ending badly and that felt strangely liberating.

Thirty minutes later I managed to make contact with a helicopter pilot who was flying off the coast. He gave me a new frequency to try and I gave him my latitude and longitude to pass onto the authorities. Then thanked him and changed frequencies to Sondestrome Information, again.

They picked up my transmission on the third attempt. My first question was what the weather was like along the coast. There'd been a layer of freezing cloud covering Nuuk earlier and it was forecast to be there all day. Impenetrable. Deadly.

Fortunately, luckily, unexpectedly, it'd moved offshore by a couple of miles. I changed my flight plan and confirmed I was diverting there.

About 30 miles out, five hours after take off, I started to spot the mountains along the coast. I felt better. The nearer I got the more the cloud started to dissipate. The occasional fluffy white thing at low level, but blue skies. A wave of such bloody relief started to wash over me.

With 10 miles to run the weather looked great. Beautiful azure blue sea. Scattered islands. Great visibility. Big yellow thing in the sky.

I could just make out Nuuk on the horizon.

Decision Height

I heard myself laugh out loud at the fact this was the only leg of my trip where the weather's changeability had, despite the forecast, actually conspired to help.

Jon Hilton

Keying the mike I called the Tower frequency and agreed to join long final. They wanted to send an air ambulance off before me so I slowed to let the other aircraft go.

Feeling relieved that my ordeal was nearly over my body started shaking. Couldn't help myself. Tremors affecting my arms and hands.

Then I began worrying about landing. The tyre issue, which I'd nearly managed to banish from my mind, resurfaced. Plus the airspeed indicator was still goosed. Frozen solid.

Cock up the landing, blow the tyre, and I could write off the aircraft. I'd have to guess my airspeeds. The key was to touch down as slowly and gently as possible, ideally right hand wheel first.

Decision Height

The airport came into view and got closer. And closer. Nuuk town centre on my left, mountains to the right. I crossed the runway threshold and stayed as slow as felt safe.

Pulled tentatively back on the stick and the nose of the aircraft started to rise ever so slightly. Throttle closed. And tried for a gentle touchdown.

Cocked things up. Misjudged my speed and flopped out of the sky like a dead duck. Horrible landing and I felt the shock through my spine.

Both tyres stayed inflated despite the bone jarring impact. So bloody, fuckingly, relieved to have made it back to some form of civilization. A small wave of euphoria made me light headed.

Taxied to the vast apron, stopped the aircraft, shut everything down, unstrapped myself and tumbled out of the India Zulu. The temperature was maybe two degrees but with the blue skies and the flood of relief I was feeling, it felt beautifully warm.

Jon Hilton

Sitting next to the aircraft I took ten minutes to enjoy being alive. I'd survived and was still breathing, but I was still thousands of miles from home.

It occurred to me that the aircraft could be taken apart and shipped back to Blighty... I'd have wimped out, but I'd be in one piece...

An hour later she was tied down and I was off to the Sailors Hostel. Cheap and cheerful, but clean. Flying finished for Saturday.

Chapter 14 - Greenland 2nd June

Sunday

Greenland doesn't like chaps flying on Sundays so I just lazed around the hostel all day. Depressingly bored.

The lady behind the reception desk was young, blonde, and Danish. Very pretty. She wanted to chat so I listened for a while to her slightly American accent.

I gave thought to walking into the town centre but had zero energy. Went for my evening meal. Went back to the room. Finally fell asleep.

Jon Hilton

Chapter 15 - Greenland 3rd June

Monday

Woke up far too early. Struggled out of bed and made my way to the sink. Leaned against it and stared into the mirror. A tired, puffy, face looked back at me. For the umpteenth time I felt desperate for a good sleep.

Checked out of the hotel at 7.30am, found a taxi and made my way into the Nuuk terminal building.

Jon Hilton

Walking through the corridors I bumped into the helicopter pilot who'd passed over the relay details on the Saturday.

He said I'd sounded quite relieved, over the radio, to hear about the previous days improving conditions. That was a damned understatement. I put on a cheerful smile and shook his hand.

Wearing one of my 'Star Trek' thermal shirts I lumped all my belongings up the spiral staircase to the Tower. The three Danish guys on duty seemed genuinely pleased to see me.

Sitting on their settee I checked the day's weather and called the Sondestrome weather station.

The concern was a spot along the coast reporting snow, freezing fog and high winds. The consensus between the four of us was that it was best to wait a day and fly on the Tuesday.

I quietly figured the flight might work out ok but it takes a certain mindset to go against local knowledge and suggestions.

Decision Height

Very tired, very frustrated. I wanted home.

With my bags strewn around the Tower, and in between aircraft landing and taking off, I spent an hour chatting. All very pleasant stuff.

For some reason the subject of Vikings, and Scandinavians in general, came up and how they'd influenced the world. I was out of my depth with that conversation and figured I'd revert to type and start teasing.

I politely informed my audience that, and not a lot of people know this, Abba are from Bolton in Lancashire. And that Hans Christian Andersen, he of the fairy stories, was born in Bury on the outskirts of Manchester.

The chaps nodded and told me that Margaret Thatcher was from outer space. I agreed that that seemed logical.

I've got to say they were great fun and genuinely nice people.

Turning my attention to the fact I wasn't going anywhere I made my way outside to check the aircraft and specifically the state of the tyre.

Cold day, but not oppressively so. Generally overcast cloud with blue skies coming and going.

The tyre definitely seemed low but it was just about inflated. It was going to go completely flat at some point, though, and sods law said it'd become a major problem.

With the temperature round about freezing I pulled my fingers out of my pockets and reluctantly started to flex them.

Jon Hilton

I wandered over to one of the Ground crew and agreed, through a mixture of broken English and gesturing, that it was ok to pull the aircraft towards one of the hangers and away from any taxiing, commercial, aircraft.

Opening the gull wing doors I started to get my tools out of the cabin.

One of the young guys looked at me as if to say, 'aren't you a pilot'. I looked back with my very best, 'I'm prepared to be helped' expression.

Five minutes later two fellas had pulled out a large tool kit and were changing the tyre. I made a show of taking off the engine cowling and pretending to know what I was looking at.

For good measure I added some oil. It'd seemed low.

Decision Height

There've been times in my life when I've been able to portray a very competent veneer, when the reality of the situation is that I've no idea what the fuck I'm doing.

Ten minutes later the tyre was fixed and the spat was back on the wheel. It'd taken them a fraction of the time it would've taken me.

Neither was fluent in English but I was invited upstairs to have a cuppa with the Fire & Rescue guys. Always good people to have a friendly relationship with.

Hence, myself and half a dozen natives sat around the crew room drinking tea and chatting, in halting English, about footie.

Jon Hilton

Humorously they were all Man United fans apart from the Supervisor who supported Arsenal. They good naturedly teased him for being stupid.

I'm a Bolton Wanderers fan, but during his youth Dad had been a season ticket holder at Old Trafford, so I went along with the mickey taking. Great fun and very nice folk.

After playing with their remote control helicopter for ten minutes, in front of a cheerful audience, I said my goodbyes and made my way back to the hostel.

My lady friend behind the counter spotted me and said, *'hey Jon'* which sounded so damned sexy the way she said it.

More of a *'heyyy, jonnn'* vibe to it.

I have to say it does make a chap feel good about himself when a young lady flirts. There was nothing more to it than that but it put a smile on my face.

Having said that I'm so completely gormless where females are concerned. She'd have had to have turned up at my door wearing slinky white underwear, at midnight, and handed me an envelope with SWALK written on it before I'd have realized what the hell she was thinking.

Anyway.

She went on to explain that my room had been taken and the only one left didn't have a bathroom. That'd mean traipsing down the hall to have a pee or shower which I wasn't looking forward to.

Still, things could have been worse.

Decision Height

Jon Hilton

Chapter 16 - Greenland
4th June

Tuesday

Woke up at 2am.

The lady next door was making loud moaning noises. Clear as a bell. I didn't think she was pleasuring herself but couldn't be sure. Something was going on and I didn't have the energy to bang on the wall.

Turning over I half wrapped the pillow around my head, and finally nodded off.

Reawakened at 5am to the sound of folk walking passed my door and muttering in Danish. Sailors getting ready for the maritime hunt.

I couldn't help but feel bloody frustrated about all the bloody noise because this was the only accommodation I'd found with blackout curtains.

In a daze I got out of bed and trudged down the hall to the shower. Washed, brushed my teeth, and dragged my feet towards the eating area.

Ambling past the reception desk I told the disinterested middle aged lady, not my young friend, that room number 1 was bloody terrible. She wasn't remotely bothered.

Decision Height

Had something to eat, checked out, and headed to the airport by taxi. Took my Proplus tablets out of my bag and stared at the box. I wasn't going to use any but it made me feel better knowing they were in there.

At the entrance to the airport I put on my, 'I belong here' face and started opening doors to find a way to get Airside. No one questioned or stopped me and I finally found a corridor leading onto the Apron.

Warmest day so far. Eight degrees centigrade felt positively bloody tropical.

I walked across the wide expanse of concrete towards Samson, unlocked both doors and put my two bags on board. Then started a slow amble around the aircraft.

There was a little bit of pink antifreeze on the nose wheel spat that'd leaked from somewhere. I reluctantly took the cowling off the engine and checked the hoses. All seemed fine. The reservoir was stocked up and still held a surplus of fluid.

This had happened before when the aircraft had stood for a day or two. I'd hoped the service in England would have cured the problem. Obviously not. Like I say the quantities that'd escaped were relatively small, though.

At the same time it's somewhat unsettling when you're a thousand or so nautical miles from any bugger with a working knowledge of a Rotax 912 engine.

I made a mental note to buy more Mars bars in the hope another sugar rush would cheer me up.

Feeling a tad uncomfortable I made my way back to the Tower, climbed the spiral stairs and met my new mates. Speaking to them yesterday they'd advised against flight. Today they were in favour.

Jon Hilton

I looked through the Tower windows and eyed up the clag above the airfield. By UK standards it wasn't legal to fly. I wasn't sure if the term existed here but figured an insurance broker or CAA executive, somewhere, would have a perspective on what represented reasonable caution.

The cloud base was below 1,000 feet and the visibility was a couple of miles. It was coming and going. Not particularly healthy but the optimist in me could see an opportunity. I stared upwards at the dense, miserable looking clouds, and experienced a sense of foreboding.

The Danes suggested the weather wouldn't improve directly above Nuuk for the rest of the day. It'd sit like a bad hat above the town, but the expectation was that 20 miles or so south it should be quite pleasant.

Decision Height

I checked with Rob in England and phoned the Sondrestrome weather station. At the same time the Tower fellas were good enough to print out a raft of Met paperwork.

Sitting on the settee I blankly stared at the paperwork trying to decide what to do, whilst also feeling sick and tired of life and death decisions.

I wanted home. Decision made, I was going. Felt too tired to sit around doing nothing.

Looking up from my collection of papers I told the three guys of my plans. They volunteered to file the flight plan on my behalf and we all shook hands. 8.20am at that point. I made my way down the stairs with my notes and file tucked under my armpit.

Fifteen minutes later I was airborne and bumping along underneath the cloud base. Nothing to be done but focus on what I could see and press on.

Jon Hilton

Ten minutes later the promised hole in the cloud appeared and I climbed into the most amazing blue. Mountains on my left. Snow covered peaks everywhere. White clouds underneath me.

I levelled out at 3,000ft and admired the panorama. Told the fella's at Nuuk I was changing frequency, said goodbye, and went over to Sondestrome Information. The new guy sounded very official and asked me to report in every 30 minutes as I flew south along the Coast.

Looking around the cabin all seemed to be working well. The fact that my clothes, immersion suit (the half I'd climbed into) and rucksacks were red was a constant reminder I wasn't in Kansas anymore, so to speak.

A standard scan of the instruments showed a problem on the Dynon. Something was flashing. The oil pressure was spiking just outside the green zone and hitting the amber arc. Shit.

Mentally I started asking myself what the practical implications would be. Would matters slowly deteriorate over a sustained

Decision Height

period of time? Or would a hose, somewhere, come loose and the engine simply die?

I considered an immediate 180 degree turn with the intent of landing back at Nuuk. Then thought, no, let's try to figure out if the problem is because of the relatively high temperature. Or other factors.

For the umpteenth time I cursed myself for being a semi literate arse from Bolton who had got so far outside his comfort zone it was bloody ridiculous. I needed thinking time.

With my bowels twitching, I sat a little more upright in my seat, and with the same throttle setting started a slow climb to 8,000ft.

Jon Hilton

The fluctuations kept spiking so I figured temperature wasn't necessarily a factor. I pulled the RPM right back and closed the throttle. Still spikes in the oil pressure.

I experimented with different power settings and put the aircraft into different attitudes. Pulling on my harness, to make sure I was firmly attached to India Zulu, I put her into a 30 degree turn. Then levelled out and banked in the opposite direction. The readings were still fluctuating which was bloody annoying because I was trying to figure out some type of pattern. Something that would allow me to limp on.

Turning south again I reached across to my smaller rucksack. Wedged the stick between my knees in an attempt to keep flying straight and level, and retrieved my Rotax book. Then started leafing through it.

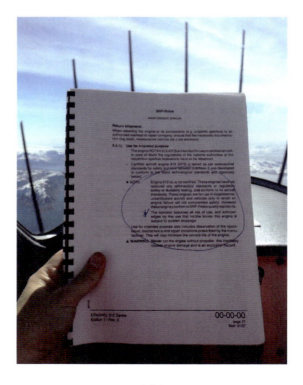

Decision Height

There's a really rewarding section in the preface that states that the engine isn't suitable for aircraft, isn't certified, and is liable to sudden stoppages. That's a charming and rewarding page to read, especially when you've nowhere to land and everywhere to crash.

The book warned of low pressure issues but nothing regards high pressure. The readings weren't red. Mostly green with lunges into the yellow arc. It played on my mind whether I should try for a forced landing in the sea, or the shoreline, if things went tits up and the engine exploded in some way.

One of the waypoints along my route was a small airstrip in the middle of nowhere. Equidistant from where I'd started and where I was heading.

A place called Pamuuit. Home to a hundred or so people. Decent sized runway, although no one seemed to fly from there other than very occasionally as a way of dropping off supplies to the natives. My file of papers warned of nasty crosswinds for those trying to land. I orbited above the runway whilst trying to figure out what to do.

My butt hole started to flap a little. Anxious but not scared.

If I made it to Narsass, I could crate the aircraft and get her shipped home. Taking a more cautious approach suggested I land on the strip 8,000ft below and figure things out there.

But if I landed and then decided to fly on, would the engine be able to handle the demands of a full power take off? And what if the damn crosswinds caused problems on landing and caught me out ?

What the fuck-a-doodle do should I do?

Jon Hilton

On the basis my head was starting to hurt I began a slow descent. Land and give up, but still be alive seemed the way to go. Maybe I could get the aircraft home and maybe I couldn't.

In a gentle downward spiral, I picked up my phone to take a few happy snaps. Holding it in my hand, at 6,500ft, the icon appeared showing it'd picked up a phone signal. Bloody amazing.

I figured it was time to contact the UK and text the chap in England who'd serviced the aircraft. Very knowledgeable, highly experienced. And asked his opinion. After orbiting for fifteen minutes the response came back that he thought it was an encroaching sensor failure. The words 'Not uncommon' formed part of his text terminology.

Like a merry go round I kept circling through 360 degrees watching the same view come and go, whilst trying to think. All the instruments were green except for the one which was playing silly buggers. I text a pilot friend of mine and he suggested a sensor issue would be the problem, too.

Feeling both anxious and uninsured the decision was to carry on south. That little reassurance felt good but didn't make the doubts go away. Cock, fuck, bollocks. The readings weren't getting worse, though. But were they the initial signs of a catastrophic failure?

I was running through different scenarios when Sondestrome called up. I cursed. I was eight minutes late for my position report. Damn. I apologised for my tardiness. The guy asked if I was operationally ok. I paused, then said yes.

For the next twenty minutes I tried to put the sensor readings out of my mind. The view was stunning. Mountains and the icecap on the horizon. I tried to blank out everything else.

Decision Height

Thirty minutes later I heard Sondestrome call up another aircraft and the controller talked about an Emergency Locator Beacon being activated. I started to pay attention.

A second aircraft was being called. There was no reply. Their ELB had been activated.... What was going on?

The suggestion was that someone had crashed and needed rescuing. Nothing had been heard since the Emergency Beacon had started transmitting. Various aircraft were being called on to search. Nothing was asked of me so I continued onwards feeling twitchy.

Was someone dying out there?

At the same time I couldn't help but feel relieved no one had wanted my help. I wasn't sure the engine would hold out but then again lives might be at stake and there was no way I'd be able to say no if they asked for my assistance.

Jon Hilton

The minutes ticked by and I quietly thanked the gods no one wanted me to fly inland and search for wreckage.

Please don't let anyone die.

I subsequently navigated the Fjords around Narsass and made my way towards safety.

Decision Height

Samson and I lined up, and landed. No drama. Got out of the aircraft and felt the heat of the sun on my face and hands. For the first time since leaving the UK it felt warm and that was a lovely sensation.

At the same time the outstanding question was whether some poor soul, or souls, were actually injured or potentially dead somewhere on the icecap. Chillingly I realised that could've been my fate.

The ground crew appeared and asked if I was going onto Kulusuk that day. Midday by then and I didn't think I'd make it before they closed at 4.45pm. Plus I was cream crackered and wanted to reflect on the oil pressure issue, so I said, 'no'.

The two guys backed up the refuelling truck and started the rigmarole of filling her up with Avgas.

For good measure they managed to slosh fuel all over the surface of the wings as they finished topping off the tanks. I just frowned at them, shook my head, and reached inside the aircraft to retrieve my sponge and begin the clean-up operation.

They seemed nice enough and I didn't want to be grumpy but couldn't help but wonder how they'd feel if I pissed over their car bonnets.

Having said that, Narsass has no real roads, is home to only a couple of hundred folk and they're not big into vehicular transport.

Feeling completely fatigued I sat in the sun, by the side of Samson, for 10 minutes. Then with one rucksack over each shoulder got up and made my way to the hotel.

Jon Hilton

It was, maybe, 300 yards from the airport and seemed like such a bloody grim, soulless, place.

I walked in to the large reception area and rang the bell. A native lady appeared and asked what I wanted.

Decision Height

I said to check in. She looked at me like it'd be a struggle to squeeze anyone in unless they'd booked in advance.

Figuring the place had a couple of hundred rooms, and maybe thirty guests, it seemed wise to both play along with her self-importance and look cheerful. Sixty seconds later she said she had a vacancy and gave me the key to my old room.

At no point on the journey had I booked any accommodation in advance. That seemed like tempting fate and each time I'd touched down I'd been prepared to sleep in the aircraft overnight. It occurred to me that I might have got more sleep if I'd roughed it.

Walking past the giant statue of a polar bear, in the foyer, I made my way to the room and crashed out on the bed. Found myself staring at the ceiling mulling over the day's events.

During the first hour of my stay I heard the infamous *'whoop, whoop'*, noise of a Huey type helicopter leave the airport.

Then return. Then leave....

I was hoping there'd be a happy ending for the lost souls out there.

Jon Hilton

Chapter 17 - Greenland 5th June

Wednesday

Woke up before 5am. Tried to sleep on and failed. Finally threw off the covers at 6.30am and made it to the shower.

Dressed, left the room behind, and walked along the corridor. Went past the 20ft tall representation of a polar bear and on towards the rather depressing restaurant.

Decision Height

On the way back to my room I bought credits for the internet from reception and managed to check the weather on my iPad. It looked like there'd be decent weather on the flight to Kulusuk but there'd be a lot of wind writhing about.

Do-able if I went immediately but later that day the conditions were expected to be north of 50 knots and that could be lethal. The need was to go immediately.

I walked the three hundred or so yards from the overpriced hotel to the airport. One of the helicopter pilots said, *"hi"* as I wandered around the terminal building. I asked his opinion about the day's weather and he said it was going to be too much for him to fly. That gave me a moment of tired reflection.

I figured there was a twenty minute window to make a final 'go, no go' decision before the wind started to pick up and became unsafe. At the moment, though, it was beautifully calm and sunny. If I got going now there might have a tough hour in the air but the rest of the trip should be good.

Made my way up to the Tower and introduced myself to the duty staff. Asked their opinion and they seemed fine about me going. I called the Greenland Weather centre, from their phone, and was told that one of their automated weather stations was already reading a 20 knot headwind at ground level. Do-able, but not necessarily pleasant or sensible at higher altitudes.

If I didn't go I'd be here for days....

Figuring that the chopper chap would have more of an insight into local conditions, and if he wasn't getting airborne then maybe I should sit tight, too.

I made my way outside onto the Apron and stared up at the crystal blue above me, and reluctantly decided to err on the side of caution.

Jon Hilton

It seemed like such a beautiful day and my desperate need was to get airborne. Felt like I was balancing my whole life on a bloody knife edge. Go or don't go ?

I slowly made my way back to the small terminal building, with a headache brewing, and asked the helicopter pilot about hangarage space. He pointed me towards the giant Air Greenland hanger. I walked across the Apron and banged on the huge sliding doors.

Hearing a noise inside, I stepped through the small inset doorway. A tall Danish chap was stood on top of a large jet engined helicopter inspecting the turbine mechanism. He was maybe 20ft off the ground.

In a slightly loud voice I asked about putting India Zulu inside and out of the forthcoming wind. He shrugged and said that would involve paperwork. I shrugged back and asked what that meant.

He said $800 per day. I shrugged again and said I thought I'd give it a miss. Plan B was to tie her down outside but I knew she'd get smashed about in the wind. Plan C meant getting the fuck out of dodge, ASAP, and try to beat the conditions. Decision made.

And then another Dane appeared, who'd overheard the conversation, and said if I bought everyone chocolate, Samson could stay safely indoors.

I decided to stay, said thank you, and shook his hand.

Leaving the hanger I walked back to the terminal, made my way to the Tower, and checked the weather again. It looked like by missing my 20 minute window I'd be stuck here for at least 2 days whilst a weather front buggered about.

Decision Height

The helicopter pilot reappeared and I mentioned my dilemma. His turn to shrug this time. Not for the first time this trip I got the impression folk were happy for me to stick around so they'd have someone new to chat too.

An hour later I'd dropped off my stash of choccy and pulled the aircraft safely indoors. Ten minutes after that I was driving to see the sights around the airfield with the chopper chap.

We visited the derelict site of the old military hospital used during the 2nd World War and the Korean War.

And just for good measure we stopped by the wreckage of two aircraft that'd crashed at the airport.

Ten minutes later we dropped by the docks.

Jon Hilton

My guide was giving me the tourist treatment and seemed happy to kill time. A subtle mention was made that the sensible

Decision Height

approach to getting home was to take the wings off India Zulu, crate her, and send her home by ship. The numbers put to that idea were £1,500 and a month or so before Samson made it back to the UK.

That seemed like quite an attractive idea but then again it'd mean I'd failed in my attempt to get home. What to do?

After being dropped off at the hotel reception I walked past the circular staircase and the Polar Bear, as a text arrived from the UK. It said my phone bill had reached £500 and the phone would no longer work unless more cash was stumped up. Typical.

Without the phone I'd have no internet access so reluctantly, and deeply pissed off, I made my way to the reception desk and asked for thirty minutes of internet credits. Then tried to pay my bill online.

Rather frustratingly the card was rejected. My blood chilled as I had a horrible feeling I'd be stranded in a foreign country without money or contact with home.

There'd be an email brewing, somewhere, saying my card was subject to suspicious activity and that's why, for my own protection, it'd been declined.

With much pleading and smiling I managed to get the hotel receptionist to let me use their landline to call MasterCard. I patiently explained to the person on the end of the phone that, yes I really was in Greenland, and yes they should unlock the card for the sake of my sanity.

I also explained, clinging to my sanity like a life raft, that I'd informed Mastercard of my trip before I left the UK and this shouldn't have happened. The lady on the phone wasn't remotely interested.

Jon Hilton

Twenty minutes later the problem was resolved and I made it back to my room. Then stooged around for hour upon hour, climbing the walls.

There was a TV in the room that only seemed to pick up American, 'home make over' programmes. Watching half a dozen sets of kitchens and bathrooms being replaced and revamped isn't as exciting as you might think. Time slowed.

I could hear the wind picking up outside the building as an insistent howling noise permeated into the room.

Chapter 18 - Greenland 6th June

Thursday

Ate breakfast and went back to the room. Incredulously bored, mind numbingly so. Very blowy outside and I could hear it pushing against the building as 50 knots said hello.

I decided to wander over to the aircraft and check her health. Putting on my fleece I walked outside and struggled to stand upright in the face of the gale.

Adopting a walk that meant leaning my body forwards to counteract the force against me, for some reason, I had a huge smile on my face.

Made it to the Terminal building and bought more chocolate for my new friends, then went airside towards the huge hanger.

Jon Hilton

India Zulu was sat in the back right hand portion of the open space behind another jet engined helicopter. No one else there.

Standing in front of the Microlight, whilst tucking into a Mars, my eyes roamed all over her looking for anything that might be amiss. The first thing that struck me was more antifreeze splattered on the nose wheel spat. Fuck.

I don't like it when an aircraft leaks. My OCD dislikes untidiness and finds it annoying.

Feeling guilty for being in the hanger I decided to quickly check the aircraft and get out before anyone appeared and suggested my presence was making the place look untidy.

Taking the cowling off the engine I started to poke my head around the workings of the beast. The key thing seemed to be that everything looked clean. Which I took to be a good sign.

One of the anti-freeze hoses felt suspiciously moist and I strapped a cable tie around the blighter to tighten it.

Decision Height

Reassuringly there was still enough antifreeze in the reservoir to see me home, I hoped. Hopefully the leak wasn't a big deal. Hopefully.

Reattaching the thin carbon fibre cowling I sat on the concrete floor and looked up at Samson. It felt strange knowing that an inanimate object was all that stood between me and disaster.

Whilst unwrapping a Kit Kat Chunky my mind started to wander and I began pondering why people give things names. Squatting on the cold surface, with my butt cheeks twitching, I realised it's because we want them to like us.

A maintenance fella appeared and I introduced myself. Like all the Danish guys he seemed very pleasant. Didn't in any way seem bothered I was milling about, so I figured I'd stick around.

He pointed me to one of the rooms, off the main hanger, and suggested making a brew. Ten minutes later, cup of tea in hand, I was stood in front of Samson wondering whether to tackle the lack of airspeed readings.

Jon Hilton

With water and previously ice in the pitot tube there were readings above 70knots but nothing below. Hence no numbers to help me land and I was flying by feel.

Apart from nearly crashing at Nuuk I'd handled things reasonably well but it was only a matter of time before a cock up came calling.

Especially having been faced with winds coming from both ends of the runway at Narsass, elements of windshear, sensor headaches, escaping antifreeze fluid, ice and fatigue... it made sense to try to resolve the ASI problem and get that working again. One less headache for the future.

That meant draining the pitot system. The teeny tiny problem was that I'd seen the process done twice but never actually done it myself.

It involves 'taking off' the main instrument panel. You're then presented with the back of the Dynon, the piece of kit that tells you everything you need to know. That has three output jacks.

You disconnect the correct one, get out of the aircraft and walk to the pitot tube in the wing. Then blow down it to clear the rain water out of the tubing.

Unfortunately I wasn't 100% sure which output jack was bloody well which. The dilemma was that I'd potentially lose all data if I guessed wrong. Flying without altitude information and airspeed readings would be problematic. Russian roulette whilst you're thousands of miles from a maintenance facility or responsible adult.

With my brew going cold I text a couple of knowledgeable chaps in England to reassure myself I'd be doing it right. I figured it was the cable with the red tag. Twenty minutes later two texts had arrived saying they 'thought' that was correct.

Decision Height

Feeling like a bomb disposal expert I wrapped an extra piece of towelling around the disconnected tube in the aircraft cabin, walked to the wing and started blowing from the pitot end.

Nothing came out and I tried again. And again. Then felt very light headed and decided to sit down on the concrete.

The last time I'd seen water removed from the pitot system the guy had used an air compressor and now I understood why he'd used that piece of kit. Standing on tip toes I blew harder into the tube.

Feeling like my head would explode I went very dizzy and sat down on the hanger floor, again. Then got up and went for a sit down inside the aircraft, head spinning.

My gaze cast over the towel and there was a certain amount of moisture on it. Mission accomplished. Brain injury and embolism avoided. Thank fuck for that. I reattached everything and left the hanger vowing to never, ever, do that again.

The evening meal at the hotel was boring. No one to talk to. The hotel TV was useless and I was bloody fed up with American dream bathrooms and concrete work tops.

I decided to check out in the morning and try the hostel a quarter mile up the road.

Chapter 19 - Greenland
7th June

Friday

Same routine, woke up too early, showered and made my way to breakfast. Perpetually tired. Looked at the weather again on my iPad and realised there was no chance of flying. Stupidly windy everywhere along my route to Kulusuk.

Checked out of the hotel and lugged my stuff to the airport and spent a little time with my helicopter friend.

We sat in his small office and chatted about nothing in particular. Tax rates in Denmark, the nature of the relationship between the natives and the Danes, life as a pilot.

From what I could tell, Greenland relies heavily on Denmark for its infrastructure, intellectual management and funding.

However since reserves of Gold, Oil and Uranium were now being found in the country that was adding a new dimension to the relationship. The suggestion was that if significant amounts of minerals were found, the Danes would be booted out by the soon to be self-sufficient natives.

Human nature is such a constant in the world that an ironic smile crept across my face.

We idly talked about various things and he invited me to play pool in the evening at the only pub. I spent an hour in his office simultaneously making small talk and trying to complete a crossword on my iPad.

There was a giant map on the wall and in a bored, disinterested, way I asked about the black lines linking some of the fjords. They seemed to be in the areas I'd flown through.

The reply was, *'they're electricity cables slung from the valley sides. Suspended at 1,000ft. Won't be on your GPS or maps'.*

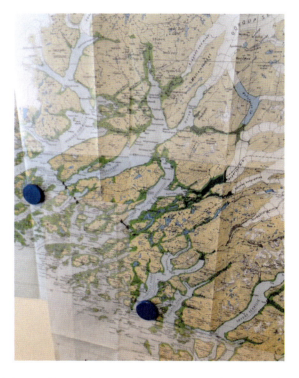

I would have flown just under or over them. And narrowly missed being garrotted at the same time. I said, *'oh'*. And felt my bum hole constrict.

Jon Hilton

Five minutes later, as my head was still spinning, another Danish chap popped his head round the doorway. He said hi, and suggested a pool tournament would be a good idea for the evening.

There was a chance of flying the following day and a late night, with beer, didn't seem like a clever idea. Probably what I needed, but not a smart thing to do.

Plus the bar only opened at 10.30pm and on the basis it was simply open one day a week, everyone got absolutely slaughtered, apparently.

Shortly afterwards I was hauling my kit the 1/4 mile to the hostel. Walking against the ever present gusting winds meant lurching forward, as I plodded on.

Decision Height

Opening the door I was met by a couple of young folk. PHD students, two Brits and a Canadian. The lack of a TV meant myself and the three of them were duty bound to chat away the hours.

I learnt about the amount of ice melting on the Greenland icecap each year (200 billion tonnes) and the state of play with the French community in Canada.

And then as the evening came around we started to play some damn silly 'triangle' game. With me being the stooge trying to figure out the rules.

Bloody confusing process and I had zero idea what was going on. Excellent fun though, and it seemed I was being initiated into a new gang.

It was then I was introduced to Jagermeister. Only the one shot but it went down like a Russian Cossack.

Jon Hilton

Unfortunately I couldn't get it out of my mind that the clock was ticking for me to get out of Danish airspace before my pseudo visa expired.

That screwed up my ability to relax and I reluctantly said goodnight to my chatty friends and wandered off to my executive accommodation. Midnight by then.

I'd really enjoyed their company and the friendly banter felt like the real highlight of the trip.

Great people. A credit to their universities.

Decision Height

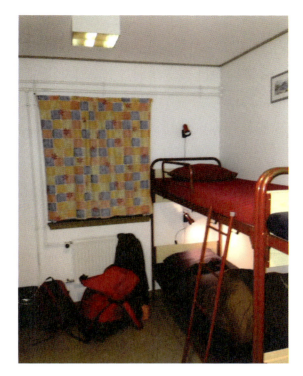

Chapter 20 - Greenland, Iceland 8th June

Saturday

Woke up in the hostel at 4.30am with daylight pouring through the window. The sleeping bag was bloody uncomfortable. I couldn't help but think there was a certain amount of residual dandruff attached to the pillow that definitely, definitely didn't belong to me.

Tried to fall back to sleep without any great success. At 7am I got up and made my way to the communal shower area. None of the guys were awake so I mentally wished them great lives and thirty minutes later found myself at the airport.

Decision Height

Checked the weather again from the office. It seemed better than the previous days, decent at Narsass, good at Kulusuk. A weak Occluded front off the coast but that didn't seem like it would particularly affect me. Maybe I'd clip an area of poor weather if I was unlucky.

Juggling the conditions over the course of hundreds of miles really gives a chap a headache. Not for the first time my brain started to ache with all the different scenarios that could be encountered.

My helicopter mate thought it was the best day to go but the responsible adult in the Tower wasn't so sure. Rob in England thought it'd be a reasonable flight and he'd even filed my flight plan.

I was dog tired and conscious of not pushing any situation that could spiral out of control. Folk die because of 'get home itus' where they take poor decisions based on a desire to get home for tea and crumpets.

At the same time I was on a timeframe to get out of Danish airspace and wanted to both see Dad before his heart op and catch up with my beautiful little, smiley faced, daughter.

Looking through all the Met data again, both on my iPad and the print outs, I thought sod it, I'm going. Should be do-able. If I didn't go I'd be here for a week waiting out the weather.

After a certain amount of faffing about I pulled the aircraft out of the giant Air Greenland hangar. 9am by then. A calm morning offering a certain optimism that the worst of the weather had passed in the night.

I struggled into the lower half of my giant red condom, climbed aboard, called for taxi instructions, and took off.

Jon Hilton

The electricity cables slung across the fjords were playing on my mind a little. At 110 miles an hour there was no way I'd see them until I'd been surgically removed from my head.

Miraculously a Kit Kat Chunky appeared in my hand. I kept scanning outside whilst checking the instruments and simultaneously tearing the wrapping off with my teeth. Breakfast was at hand and I was determined to eat it without being decapitated.

We flew south, to the very tip of Greenland, before heading north again and following the coast as per my flight plan.

Decision Height

The weather started to turn. I was half expecting it, sod's law. The winds picked up and at 5,000ft there was an unpleasant 25 knots of headwind to contend with.

That felt like I was walking and it was going to affect my earlier presumptions on flight time.

My left hand was gently holding onto the stick, my right was gripping the centre console. All I could hear was the throbbing of the engine through the headset. Here we go again.

The temperature was falling. The winds were getting angry. Samson and I were faced with another under or over decision as a solid wall of white appeared.

This time I opted for underneath the clouds and called Sondestrome to report my position and state my intention to follow the coast.

Jon Hilton

The mist rolled in and we involuntarily started descending to the height of the cliffs. More areas of ice started to show along the coast.

Mountains denoting the difference between the water and the land. No emergency sites to put down. I was forced lower. Murk everywhere. A kind of milky white look to everything. Very poor visibility, a lot less than a mile.

Started to spot small icebergs. Forced lower again. Couldn't maintain a track along the coastline without constant anxiety about hitting something in the treacherous conditions. Rain began striking the aircraft and I thought, 'oh fuck'.

Decision needed.

Stay attached to the coast with the vague possibility of a successful crash landing or take a more direct track over the ocean towards Kulusuk. Or I could turn round but there were no guarantees in that direction either.

Decision Height

I was numb to the whole dying thing as my eyes kept flicking to the Dynons clock. The minutes ticked by. I altered course and took a more North Easterly track over the water. That took me away from land and hopefully removed the prospect of colliding with anything, such as a small island, out of the equation.

The only worry then would be icebergs and ice forming on the wings.

I started making calls on various frequencies trying to get a relay message to Sondestrome information. The intent was to let them know I'd amended my flight plan.

Yet again, the soul destroying desolation of making radio calls that no one replies too. The Greenland authorities don't have radar and I was on my own. No way to sugar coat it, zero chance of recovery.

Water streamed against the windscreen as Samson flew straight and level. My head kept swivelling left and right looking for ice

Jon Hilton

on the wings. I had a continuing anxiety that the engine might fail and I kept eyeing the oil pressure gauge.

Flying at sea level the thought popped into my mind, 'if there's a chap stood up on a rowing boat then my wheels are going to take his bloody head off'... That's too damn low. Maybe a seconds worth of visibility. Intense.

I couldn't climb into the mist because ice was lurking ready and waiting for me. The only option was to fly over the water, and concentrate.

Gentle inputs to the stick and throttle. Constantly looking outside but briefly scanning the instruments for any problems. I'd become worryingly adept at nursing the engine through the cold and juggling the throttle against the engine temperatures.

It gives you something to do other than panic. Felt dog tired.

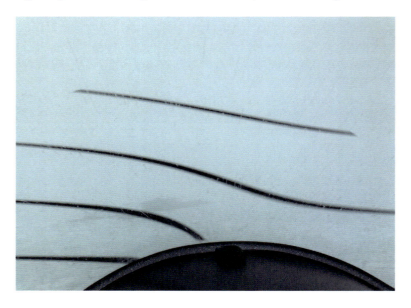

The thought slowly went through my mind, 'push the stick forward Johnny Boy and in a moment all this will be over'...

Decision Height

I wanted it to end. The pressure, the tiredness, the anxiety.

Mentally slapping myself, I acknowledged death was lurking nearby, but figured I'd have a stab at putting it off as long as possible. Minute by minute, hour by hour, I kept trying to focus.

Two lonely hours later, and about 2 hours from Kulusuk, the cloud started to lift and we were able to climb.

Firstly to 200ft and then to the luxury of a thousand feet and beyond. I called on the radio not expecting anyone to answer. The lady at Sondestrome replied, I gave her my position and confirmed everything was operationally ok. She didn't seem too bothered about me.

Climbing to 7,000ft the skies were a beautiful blue. There was a soft blanket of cloud beneath Samson's wheels.

I didn't have great faith in the weather forecasts but as long as the clouds didn't exceed 12,000ft above the water I should be fine.

Jon Hilton

The anxiety then would be how to descend into Kulusuk. It was supposed to be reasonably pleasant there. Not windy and good visibility.

Worst case I'd have to dive like a Stuka through clouds filled with ice crystals, aim vertically straight down, and see what happened. As a distraction I started flicking through the screens on the Dynon and mentally started figuring out the point we'd run out of fuel.

Generally moving closer to my destination a Mars seemed in order. And then I thought fuck it, I'll have two.

The clouds seemed to be sliding down towards the airport so I gently descended with them. Keeping more power on than normal to keep the engine warm.

Not expecting an answer, but wanting to hear my own voice, I called Sondestrome. No reply. I tried Kulusuk.

Decision Height

'Kulusuk Information, this is Golf Charlie Golf India Zulu, 20 miles to the South West of your position request joining information, please'.

My young friend answered sounding very professional. He reported the wind was 3 knots. Scattered cloud at 5,000ft. Runway, one one. The pressure setting was 1008 and he stated the runway was composed of gravel.

It sounded like he'd passed through his training period and was now a fully-fledged Tower chap. All very professional. And not really the friendly voice I'd been hoping to hear.

As standard procedure I heard myself repeat the runway and pressure details and confirmed that I'd report right base approaching via the open sea. He then said I could land from the other direction if I preferred.

I bloody hate it when someone says that. You've travelled a long way. You're mentally drained. You've been given the runway. The wind is minimal. The approach from the other side is more complicated with mountains abounding and you've already gone through the mental processes for one approach... And then the bugger suggests something else.

'I'll stick with the original plan', I said.

At the same time I started to question everything. How much of a difference will three knots make? Should I change runways? Will there be any buffeting from the mountains? Why has he put forward the suggestion? What local knowledge has he got? Has someone else had problems?

Annoyingly all my Mars bars had been munched and I found myself biting into a Kit Kat Chunky.

The clouds started to dissipate and I spotted the sea again. Then spotted the town and started to feel a little safer.

Jon Hilton

As a function of slowing the aircraft, the airspeed indicator stopped working. There'd be masses of rain water in the pitot system that'd render it useless at slower speeds.

The grey line of the runway came into view, I lined up on final approach made a few guesses as to my speed and tentatively put her wheels onto the gravel. Gentle touch down.

Decision Height

Six hours flying had reached an end. An hour or so longer than expected, but hey ho. Drained, cold and a little miserable, but still breathing. Got out, stretched, took my leggings off and walked to the Tower.

Climbed the steps and found my friend. He'd got a new supervisor and they both seemed more officious than I was expecting.

Apparently they'd been tracking me on my Spot GPS system and the device had given up the ghost half way along the trip. Folk thought I'd crashed. They'd phoned the UK to say that contact had been lost and were considering sending out Search & Rescue, when I'd reported in.

The familiar thought went through my mind that by the time they'd got round to actually doing anything it'd be to retrieve the corpse of a long dead popsicle. C'est la vie.

Not knowing what to say I just shrugged and apologised if I'd caused any problems.

I was politely told to change batteries on the tracker. It didn't need it, and I was too tired to say it wasn't a very reliable device, but I fished out my spares and did as requested.

They asked if I was staying the night and I thought, 'there is no bloody, fucking, mother of all cocks, way am I staying here'.

What I heard myself say was, *'I think I'll push on, thanks'*.

The weather from Greenland to Iceland had a front in the way. The longer term forecast suggested this was my window to get back to the UK. Fly on or wait a week.

Rob had already filed a flight plan for me. He seemed to think it was do-able. I paid my fuel bill, landing fee and purchased a dozen calorie enriched chocolate bars. Then said my goodbyes,

Jon Hilton

shook hands and slowly walked back to the aircraft and reluctantly got in.

Kulusuk to Akureyri

Started the engine, released the brakes, and began to taxi on the uneven surface. The runway was at the end of the parking area and I experienced a moment where I wasn't sure which bloody way to turn. Left or right ?

I'd look such a damn fool if India Zulu was pointing in the wrong damn direction.

Fatigue becoming increasingly evident I guessed correctly, then rolled to the runway threshold. Turned the aircraft around and lined up. Decided to get her off the gravel and stones ASAP and that meant a soft field take off.

'*Golf India Zulu ready for departure.*' Clearance was given. I pushed the throttle forward but held her on the brakes. Engine noise increased. Extra vibration in the cabin. Released the brakes and began accelerating.

I could feel the gravel runway through the seat of my pants and pulled the stick back to get the nose wheel of the ground as quickly as possible. I kept pulling to get the main wheels off the deck as Samson lumbered into the air like drunken goose. Clinging to flight we levelled out and flew five feet above the runway, whilst building up airspeed.

Ungainly take off completed I hoped to the gods the gravel hadn't given me a puncture to deal with in Iceland.

Heading east the weather cleared up, still clouds around, but the sun came out. Despite feeling unbelievably tired, the sight of the big yellow ball cheered me up.

Decision Height

Then the damn thing disappeared.

An hour later I saw the weather front. An under or over decision, again. No real logical thought involved, simply decided to stay low.

The ice covering the sea started to break up and I became more cheerful as it felt slightly warmer inside the cabin.

The ocean looked smooth and not quite as deadly as it'd seemed earlier. According to my Garmin I was barrelling along at 105 knots with one hundred feet between me and the surface of the North Atlantic.

Flat sea. No real waves. Vaguely pleasant.

Jon Hilton

I celebrated leaving Greenlandic waters with my favourite chocolate bar.

The clouds started to break up and I pushed the throttle forward, gently pulled the stick back and India Zulu started climbing. And climbing.

I'd lost radio contact with everyone by then and by gaining height it seemed possible I could speak to someone. Even if it was just another relay report via an aircraft 30,000ft above me the intent was to let folk know where I was.

Decision Height

My earlier cheerful perspective on life started to dissipate as it got colder in the cabin.

I started to make radio calls and became disheartened when no one answered after the fourth call. Tried to put a brave face on it.

My flightplan had said 5,000ft but that had gone out the window long ago in favour of staying alive. I was floating above the cloud at 9,000ft. Beautifully blue above me. White cotton wool below. The OAT sensor said it was bloody cold. After the morning's exertions I felt reasonably safe at height.

The Dynon was still suggesting high oil pressure but I'd mentally tuned that out. For the most part.

I heard chatter on the radio. I keyed the mike and called Iceland Radio. A Russian sounding lady answered and for some reason I got the impression she was a trainee. I gave her my latitude and longitude, aircraft type and my flight level. She asked if I wanted IFR clearance for a flight level of 090 across the Atlantic.

195

Jon Hilton

I said, *'yes, but you need to know I'm a VFR only aircraft and need to be able to vary my route and altitude as required'*. That confused her. She said she'd request official clearance for me.

Ten minutes later, two things happened. Firstly, the cloud started to dissipate. Still overcast but falling away from me. I would normally have descended, to keep warm, but didn't because I'd told her where I was and if I lost height I figured I'd lose contact.

The second thing was that my lady friend reported that I wasn't cleared for 9,000ft and that I had to descend below 5,500ft and report in when I hit that level.

In general terms I'd experienced more icing issues than Mr Whippy and seriously considered saying I needed to set my own level and she could go sod off. I mentally shouted abuse at her, and when that was out of my system, I keyed the mike and politely agreed to do as requested.

There was no way I was descending into cloud but we could manage the 'five, five' figure if I jinked around certain sections of the white fluffy stuff. Not ideal.

Everyone I'd heard on the radio had been up at 30 odd thousand feet. Pilots were bartering with Air Traffic for an extra 1,000ft or so. Very interesting to hear and I assumed it was an engine efficiency thing.

There were relay calls going on between pilots, ping pong style, which reinforced the fact I was in the North Atlantic black hole. And that even commercial jets couldn't always contact the ground stations.

Conscious of maintaining the Cylinder Head Temperatures, and not shock cooling the engine, I started what seemed like a gentle, managed, descent towards the clouds.

Decision Height

Ten minutes later I was at 5,500ft. Blue skies above. The cloud had evened out and we were skimming above cotton wool. Beautiful, surreal experience, but with that familiar tinge of, 'I'm scared, I'm out of my comfort zone, I'm relying on one engine that isn't certified for aviation use. And I'm uninsured'.

Plus the oil pressure readings were still out of spec' which isn't an especially healthy or wholesome feeling. And that was getting my heart pumping.

Just for good measure I hit 5,000ft and made my call. Humorously no one answered. The consideration was to climb again but I decided to stay put. Difficult thought process. Risk getting in trouble or be too low to make radio contact if help was needed.

Sod it I'd flown much, much lower and ran so many risks. No point getting overly twitchy. I frowned and felt my bum hole involuntarily clench for the hundredth time.

I called again and surprise, surprise, no answer. I had a couple of frequencies and started cycling through them trying to make contact.

Jon Hilton

Strange sensation making blind calls. You're doing it because it's the sensible thing to do. At the same time the act of making the call is soul destroying when you mentally accept there's no one there to help.

I called and called. On my sixth call a jet up at 35,000ft said hello. The chap volunteered to make a relay transmission and I gave my lat, longs and level. All seemed fine and the pilot volunteered to pass the information onto Iceland Radio.

Maybe an hour later I made contact with Reykjavik Approach. The fella sounded abrupt. He mentioned my previous conversation with the lady controller. Said I hadn't had permission to climb earlier and he was going to write an incident report that he'd latterly file with the UK CAA. The suggestion was that I'd get an official reprimand.

My initial reaction was, *'oh fuck'*. Over the radio I said, 'acknowledged'. Thirty minutes later I'd written up my thoughts on the back of a weather chart, in pencil, as preparation for a telling off.

Shortly afterwards he came back on the radio, sounding pleasant, and mentioned that it'd be touch and go whether I'd make it to Akureyri before they closed at 10pm.

He said there'd be a charge for landing even a minute after hours. I was tired but me being me I asked how much the cost would be. He asked what currency I wanted to use. Dollars, Euros or Pounds.

I said pounds but he gave me the figure in dollars. $300.00

The suggestion was that the weather was good at Reykjavik, it was 30 minutes closer, and there was no risk of a surcharge. I asked him to read out the weather. Very little wind, good ceiling and decent visibility.

Decision Height

No prospective dramas. I said I was happy to change destination and asked him to amend my Flight plan. I also mentioned the 'incident', said I'd written up my notes, and that I'd like to discuss matters face to face.

I'd been using my best, 'I'm a 747 pilot voice' and in return he'd started to sound quite amiable. He agreed to meet me when I landed. My stomach started to churn at the idea of a confrontation.

Samson and I, together with my scribbled thoughts, got closer to Reykjavik. The skies cleared and I started to feel better. Worst case I'd get told off, best case I'd still be alive.

From previous chats with folk I'd been told Reykjavik is relatively easy to get in and out of. It's on the coast with not much high ground around. I felt ok. Nervous and on edge, but ok.

Ten minutes later my new friend warned me about a mountain along my route and that I was cleared to climb above 14,000 thousand feet.

The thought struck me that he had no bloody idea what a CT was capable of.

I replied that I was unable to climb to that altitude and that I'd skirt round the obstacle. I already knew the big bugger was there.

I sidled past it at 4,000ft. The top was obscured in cloud.

Jon Hilton

At that point I entered a very large bay, of sorts. 70 miles across. It's the boundary between the Approach frequency and the airport itself. I was passed onto the Tower for landing instructions.

Briefly looking outside the cabin I could see a few more clouds lurking around. Reaching forward with my right hand I changed radio frequencies. Prepared what I wanted to say, and hit the microphone.

The lady controller confirmed the runway, winds, and that Reykjavik International had just become an IFR only airport. Not suitable for my aircraft.

The weather had deteriorated. The clouds were as low as 300ft, visibility was poor, and the wind had picked up.

Decision Height

Inside the aircraft I just acknowledged the situation. Par for the course. Taking up Golf seemed like a good option after this.

No choice but to carry on. No fuel to divert elsewhere. She asked if I wanted to switch to two other runways, which would give me a better handle on the wind.

I looked at my charts and said I'd stick with the existing plan. It meant a 15 knot direct crosswind but I was comfortable with that.

Beyond the legal limits for the aircraft but so bloody what.

The runway I'd originally been given was perpendicular to the coast hence it was straight in from the sea. No messing around.

Jon Hilton

No high buildings or ground to worry about. Just fatigue in the cockpit and a damn tired pilot.

I could see the airport beacons flashing in the distance. The vision of a couple of folk with binoculars, searching the skies from the Tower, came to mind. I wanted them to see me.

Jinking around a few clouds I completed my descent to 1,000ft and still had the airport in sight. The occasional swathe of cloud encompassed the aircraft but after everything I'd gone through that felt fine. Just hold your nerve a little bit longer, Johnny.

Moving the stick to the left, I applied a little rudder and turned from base to final approach. Lined up.

The airspeed Indicator was dead again so I had to guess the speed and focus on the runway. So tired. I noticed the Fire & Rescue truck moving to the side of the runway with its lights flashing. A jaded smile appeared on my face as it dawned on me that someone thought I might fumble the landing. Bloody pessimists.

Allowing for the crosswind I kicked in the rudder and landed without incident. No big deal. Taxied to my exit from the runway. Waved to the Rescue chaps in my most nonchalant manner and was directed to a parking slot.

Shut the engine down and sat in the aircraft for five minutes just chilling out. Leaned my head back and closed my eyes. 4hours 40 minutes of exhaustion kicked in.

Three chaps came along to say hi. Two Customs and the FBO representative. The pair of authority figures seemed more curious about the aircraft than wanting to check for contraband. Each of the trio got a Mars bar.

Finding myself sitting on the tarmac, with my immersion suit half on and half off, a feeling of numbness washed over me.

Decision Height

Another fella appeared. Cheerful looking. He introduced himself as the Approach controller I'd spoken to earlier. He looked down at me as I was on the floor. I looked up at him and handed him my notes on the whole 9,000ft incident. A nearly wordless exchange at that point.

He walked round the aircraft with a somewhat confused look on his face. I stood up and pre-empted the conversation by saying, *'it was either climb above the clouds or die'*. Which was how I felt.

He said, *'no problem, you did what you had to do and I don't think I need take this any further'*.

I got my arse off the floor and stood up. Then gave him my most cheerful smile, plus a relieved hug, and topped off the mutual friendliness by giving him my last Kit Kat Chunky.

An hour later the aircraft was tied down. I'd been given aircrew discount in the adjoining 4 star hotel and found myself eating a plastic wrapped sandwich in my room. An hour had disappeared by transiting the North Atlantic. My midnight was now 11pm local.

I reluctantly hand washed a bunch of clothes, laid them out to dry, got in bed and flaked out.

One more day and I could be home. See Ava and check how Dad was doing before he went under the knife.

Chapter 21 - Iceland, Faroes, Scotland 9th June

Sunday

The curtains weren't quite as good as I would have liked. The best so far but my eyes were open when the sun came up at 4 or 5am.

I tried to sleep on but it was one of those, 'I'm drained, very tired, and this isn't really topping me up', sleeps.

At 7am I got out of bed. Struggled into the shower, packed my damp clothes, and was eating breakfast at 7.30am. It felt so much better being part of the Icelandic tourist community. A whole hell of a lot better than I'd been used to.

By 8am I'd checked out. Thinking the Faroe Islands shut at 4pm there was a need to get my butt in gear. I wasn't 100% sure about the day's weather but my timeframe for leaving Danish Airspace was limited to that day.

I was worried about the consequences of poor decisions and ongoing fatigue. Any flight would be a gamble and there was another weather front, just to the east of Iceland, that I needed to factor in.

Probably for all the wrong reasons I decided to go. Just couldn't bear the idea of checking into the hotel again and stooging around for days whilst the weather played games.

Jon Hilton

And then having to reapply to Denmark to fly through the Faroes'.

The flight would be unpleasant for a while but then I'd be clear. No more freezing temperatures to contend with and then good, high pressure, over the UK to see me home.

From 8.30am to 10am I was alternately fiddling around with the aircraft and buzzing around the FBO office checking and re-examining the Met reports. At the same time, if all went to plan, I needed to email off my UK GAR forms to the UK authorities and getting WIFI access wasn't quite as straight forward as I might have liked.

One of the reasons to change destinations to Reykjavik was to avoid the $300 charge Akureyri charged for late opening. With a glorious tint of humour the FBO service at Reykjavik cost an additional $300 which is why ferry pilots stay away from there. Swings and roundabouts.

Decision Height

Nothing to be done but project a strained smile and hand over Mr MasterCard.

By that point I was mentally rushing through things. The chap, who was very friendly, couldn't sort out the printed invoice so I said I'd check the aircraft one more time and come back to settle the bill. In truth, as nice as he was, he was driving me insane (admittedly it's not a long commute) and I needed air.

Ten minutes later I was happier. Nipped back, paid, and got my receipt. Then climbed aboard India Zulu and started the engine. The clock was ticking and I needed to go.

The Rotax was warming up to temperature, prop' spinning, when the young guy came out of the office and headed to the aircraft, carrying my Spot GPS tracker.

Like a dimwit, and in my haste, I'd left it behind. I made a mental note not to be in too much of a hurry. Shutting the engine down I sheepishly got out and both thanked him and apologised at the same time. Fuck.

Standing by the side of Samson I took a deep breath. Then another. Getting back onboard I strapped myself in and got out the AIP notes on the airport. Reykjavik is a decent sized airport that caters for jet aircraft, so not an ideal place to make a fuck up.

I studied the airfield plates and tried to figure out the likely taxiway route. Wrote down all the radio frequencies I might be asked to use, and then called the Tower for taxi instructions.

Twenty minutes later we were airborne. The skies overcast at a couple of thousand feet and flying at 1,500ft seemed to be the order of the day.

Jon Hilton

I couldn't take a direct track along my route because of the low cloud v's mountains conundrum, hence headed south.

The Air Traffic Controller asked that I call the military to gain clearance through one of their zones. Mention was made that on a Sunday it probably wouldn't be active, with people shooting at each other, but best to call.

I changed frequencies and called. No one answered. And the Reykjavik Tower frequency couldn't pick me up when I tried to change back to them. A familiar Deja-vu feeling surfaced.

By then I was in a box valley. Hills on either side with misty cloud covering the tops. We were flying below 1,000ft and scud running again. I could see the sea further on but it was like peering underneath a curtain.

Decision Height

The aircraft had been very stable prior to entering the valley but she was being bounced around forcibly, now.

The weather gods seemed unhappy. It wasn't wings falling off time, but it did have a lose my breakfast vibe to it. Like being kicked by a donkey every couple of seconds.

Ten minutes later we were running along the coast with a strong headwind pegging our progress. I'd expected the delay but had thought it'd be further out to sea. The cloud was overcast above me and I couldn't climb above it.

Everything had looked good at Reykjavik. Good visibility and higher cloud, but 20 miles south was a different matter. Plus no one was answering on the radio and that makes you feel a little desperate.

Not for the first time I realised how desperately lonely it is flying long distances as a solo pilot.

Jon Hilton

I started recycling radio frequencies again but at 1,000ft with higher peaks around, my expectations weren't high. I tried my damnedest to sound professional, each time I keyed the mike, but there was an element of pleading with someone to answer.

The coast had a dark volcanic look to it. Black beaches. Flat countryside with farms dotted around. The cloud base was low and I was pushing a 20 knot headwind.

Thirty minutes later the panorama was bleak and I was being bounced around. The seat belt buckles were coming loose with each jolt. I was flying with one hand on the stick and the other across my chest keeping the belts tight.

Me, Samson and her contents were running along at 500ft. I wasn't feeling good about myself.

Decision Height

The visibility started to deteriorate. Maybe a mile's view. I could see the Atlantic on my right and dark scenery on the left.

Everything green had long since disappeared. There was a gothic, bleak, panorama with an element of haze blurring the distinction between the sea and the volcanic shore line.

I was looking out to sea on the right side of the aircraft, and cursing. The aircraft took a hell of a kick.

The belts weren't as tight as they should have been. I was bounced upwards, against the door, and into the bulkhead. Reaching up to my forehead I felt something warm on my fingers. Tiredness had been my overwhelming feeling but the sight of my blood made me more alert. Wide awake.

Looking straight ahead I could see the headland appearing out of the gloom.

I'd thought it was more of black beach but it wasn't. We were flying towards a rock face at 90 miles per hour. Only 300 yards

Jon Hilton

away. Oh fuck. I banked sharply right in a tight 60 degree turn, felt the blood rush to my ankles, and careered towards the open sea.

The thought on my mind was to turn back. I wanted to get home, though. I wanted to see Dad & Ava. I wanted to get through the Faroe's airspace on time and didn't want to disappoint the Danes.

I pulled the harnesses tight and rubbed my fingers across the open cut on my forehead. And carried on. The cloud forced Samson lower. It started raining and water streamed against the windscreen in front of my face.

I didn't want to risk climbing through the cloud to get away from the conditions. There shouldn't be icing issues but how deep was the cloud? Would we have to climb blind through 500ft of cloud or 5,000ft?

The lesser of two evils kept me at 20 to 30ft for about an hour. Time inched by. Visibility of 200ft. Feeling thoroughly numb, my hands were gripping the stick and throttle harder than ever before.

My eyes kept picking out the individual ripples on the surface of the North Atlantic. Droplets of water committed suicide against India Zulu and lines of rain streaked up the windscreen creating a feeling of light headed hypnosis.

The thought went through my mind, 'I hope there's no bloody boats in my path, or we're all done for'.

I managed to wriggle one arm inside the immersion suit. The other was available to key the microphone and call for help. It'd be a useless exercise at this height but it made me feel better.

For the umpteenth time my mantra was, keep calm and carry on. I was questioning my sanity but a lack of sleep was

Decision Height

somehow helping me focus on just one task. Straight and level flight.

The mist lifted and India Zulu was able to climb to 300ft. That seemed ridiculously damn safe. I was half way to the Faroes' and was feeling better about matters.

There was still the prospect of the engine failing or my falling asleep to contend with but the hell with that. The expectation was better weather from here on in.

I climbed to 5,000ft and admired the view. Clouds beneath me and thin clouds above but a relatively comfortable flight beckoned.

The worst was behind me.

Jon Hilton

For good measure a jet pilot, after various unanswered calls, volunteered to pass on my longs & lats to Iceland Radio. People knew where I was again, which felt reassuring.

At some later point a switch was made to the Faroes' radio frequency and it seemed the nightmare was coming to an end.

Approaching the islands I decided against staying high. The worries about wing icing had receded but my concentration levels were dipping.

I'd avoided my stash of Pro Plus Caffeine tablets, to that point, because I wasn't sure of the down side to them. I opened a packet and swallowed 2 tablets. Any consequences, if at all, would be a later problem. I descended to 3,000ft and approached the remote chain of islands.

Doing my well-rehearsed radio calls my RT transmissions probably sounded reasonably competent and correspondingly the Air Traffic chap seemed quite pally. Twenty miles out I was

Decision Height

forced to 1,000ft. The downward trend was disconcerting but after everything before, that height seemed like a holiday.

My new friend directed me to fly along one of the Fjords. The airport was situated at the end. I was warned about wind shear and turbulence. At the entrance to the Fjord Samson was being repeatedly kicked and I was being lobbed around the cabin.

I kept my head to one side to avoid another bash and pulled the harnesses tighter.

The nasty air calmed down. The controller chirped up, at that point, to warn me about geese and the possibility of my hitting one on final approach.

I'd thought about bird strikes and decided that by preference I'd rather hit a very small wren or possibly an undersized thrush. Hitting a goose would be a reasonably terminal experience in a Microlight.

Jon Hilton

We were running below the top of the hills at that point. Water underneath me. I could see a town and the runway in the distance. Getting closer my stomach started to churn.

Reporting five miles out the controller gave a clearance to land. Houses came into focus. The runway lights started in the town itself, running along the road, directly to the airport.

Decision Height

Courtesy of water ingress my Air Speed Indicator still wasn't working. I guessed my airspeed and flew along the centreline of the runway.

Decided that instead of gently settling her onto the tarmac I'd barrel along faster than normal and literally fly her to earth.

The thought process was that if there was any turbulence I'd rather have additional airspeed on my side. It was a gamble. An uninsured gamble.

I greased the landing a good twenty knots faster than normal, maybe 60 knots. The noise from the wheels sounded wrong as we raced along. She gradually slowed to walking pace and we taxied off the runway.

There were a couple of commercial jets between me and the Avgas pumps. A BAE 146 and an Airbus. I taxied around them and asked the fella in the Tower to ensure the jets didn't start up until I'd moved. He laughed and said he'd bear that in mind.

I shut down the engine and got out. Stretched and, yet again, slapped my ears a couple of times to get normal hearing back. It felt warm outside.

The refuelling wagon drove over and ten minutes later, for the umpteenth time, I found myself reaching for my sponge to wipe surplus fuel off the wings. Then cursed the guy for not paying attention and slopping Avgas everywhere.

Glad to be alive I slowly walked over to the Tower and climbed the steps. The chap on duty seemed like a very pleasant bloke. He was watching a rerun of a Clint Eastwood film, 'the man with no name'. Great picture quality on a High Definition TV.

We chatted about flying. I'd decided to push on and was keen to pay for the fuel and go. He asked about the flight. I said it'd been an interesting 5 hours. He looked over at the aircraft and agreed it would have been.

He then called me a 'pioneer', which was a bit of an unexpectedly shocking statement.

I walked back to the aircraft feeling a bit odd. Still worried about the forthcoming flight but within touching distance of the UK and the return of my sanity. Plus upon leaving the Faroes' I'd be beyond the Greenlandic and Danish Aviation Authorities, which would be damn nice.

Circling the aircraft I started my standard check of the flaps, stabilator, baggage doors, the various split pins and the rest of the usual suspects. Generally my OCD was kicking in again. That would be the point the oil leak became obvious.

And that was a slap in the face moment. The oil was underneath the aircraft and on closer inspection it looked like it was coming from the oil vent. I walked to the front of the aircraft, opened the oil cap and dipped the oil.

Decision Height

This time it seemed fuller than normal. Previously it'd been hovering around the halfway mark. ie. healthy. Now it seemed full. I was in a rush to get going but not if it meant dying.

Five minutes later the engine cowl was off and I was checking for obvious problems. None found. The antifreeze reservoir was ok. All the hoses seemed secure. Everything looked clean.

My hypothesis was that everywhere else had been so damn cold that when I'd topped up with oil I might have over filled her a little. In that situation the excess vents itself outside. Usually.

The thought came to me that maybe the cold had somehow prevented the oil venting out. And now it was warmer the process was working normally. I wasn't sure why the oil level would read lower in the colder climes but there was an element of sense to it.

I took the view that my assumptions were logical. Too much oil might explain the sensor issue, too. The current level seemed fine. Looking at the oil smeared across the aircraft body I absentmindedly drew a couple of parallel lines in it.

Sitting inside India Zulu I managed to hook into the airport Wi-Fi signal and looked at the weather from my iPad. On the way to Scotland there was an area of high pressure and I could expect to fly at a sensible height on this leg and have more time to prepare for the ditching process.

Twenty minutes later we were airborne. Flight plan activated. I was twitchy about turbulence in the Fjords, fat geese and oil leaks that would result in engine failure. My eyes were constantly flicking to the Dynon scanning for anything abnormal.

Jon Hilton

It occurred to me that I was so used to fear I didn't know when to be properly scared anymore. Then I thought, 'shut up Hilton and do your bloody best'.

At twenty miles out I was still in contact with my friend at Air Traffic. He suggested changing frequencies but with my history of losing radio contact, and as he was still loud and clear, I said

Decision Height

I'd stick with him. He said that was fine. All said professionally but very friendly. It was like he was at Heathrow and I was a commercial pilot.

There was a mild under or over decision with respect to a shelf of approaching clouds. No higher than 5,000ft. No issues with the cold now. I wasn't worried and climbed above their reach.

Jon Hilton

The thought went through my mind that apart from the one chap at Kulusuk no one had mentioned the weight of the aircraft or made any negative use of the word 'Microlight'. Maybe I'd just got unlucky.

After changing frequencies, and bidding farewell to my Faroes' friend, I was in touch with the Brits again. The Scottish Information radio operator informed me that my destination, Wick, would be closed by the time of my arrival.

Feeling more tired by the minute, bearing in mind I'd been flying for nearly eight hours by then, I explained that I'd spoken to the airfield operator and they were happy that I landed after

Decision Height

everyone had gone home. The lady seemed confused but said ok. I asked for their telephone number in order to cancel my flight plan when I landed.

Shortly afterwards I was winging my way past the Orkneys, approaching John O' Groats, and changed frequencies to Wick knowing no one would be there.

Beautiful blue skies. Wonderful high pressure over the UK. Stunning scenery.

If mega tiredness kicked in and I fumbled the landing there'd be no one there to help me. I'd be found upside, in a wrecked aircraft, the following morning. Alternatively if I survived at least there was a chance there'd be a pub nearby and I could go get gloriously drunk.

I approached Wick airport from the North making a series of blind calls. If anyone was listening they'd have my position reports and know what was going on.

Keeping all my transmissions professional in nature I flew over the airport at 2,000ft and picked the runway to use. The windsock looked like it was blowing at about 15 knots on the ground. Nothing scary.

Jon Hilton

On my downwind leg there was a palpable feeling of euphoria that I was nearly safe and insured again. For some unfathomable reason I started to make my radio calls in a series of accents. Demob happy.

On downwind I was Scottish. On base leg I was Irish. On final I was Welsh. It all seemed to make sense and I started grinning.

Juggling airspeed and height, we landed. Too fast. No airspeed readings to use, but quite an acceptable touch down.

Decision Height

I pulled off the runway, shut down the engine and got out. And lay on the grass for ten minutes with my arms behind my head and my legs crossed, staring at the clouds rolling across the sky.

It was after 8pm local time. I'd lost an hour or two over the last couple of days and it felt like 10pm. I'd been flying for round about 8 or 9 hours.

Tied Samson down and called Scottish Information to close my Flight Plan.

So relieved. Unbelievably thankful to be alive.

Jon Hilton

With the assistance of Far North Aviation I found a hotel and checked in. Had some reheated food, hand washed some clothes and collapsed on the bed.

Chapter 22 - UK 10th June

Monday

Woken at 7.30am by a text from a friend. It felt like 5.30am. That was at least four hours earlier than I would have liked.

The suggestion was that two aircraft were going to fly up to Kirkbride in Cumbria and we'd fly back to Barton as a three ship formation.

I reluctantly got out of bed and showered. Made my way to the airport and paid for my fuel and landing fees. With a tiny bit of water to fly over and oil still venting from the aircraft I decided to wriggle into the lower half of my immersion suit.

Lovely day. I might live in a mucky, tired, part of the UK but you've got to love this country as a whole.

I took the time to take the cowling off and look round the engine. No further leaks of antifreeze. Plenty of oil. Everything looked clean.

If you ignored the oil pressure readings and lack of airspeed readings she was in great shape considering the hell I'd put her through. There were a few signs the paint was starting to crack, though, on the carbon fibre.

Said my goodbyes, made a comment about wanting the Scots to remain a part of the UK, and took off.

Wick ATC gave me a maximum height to fly at as I took a direct track south. That pretty much immediately took me over water.

Swapping to a new frequency the controller sounded damn stroppy with the half dozen aircraft he was dealing with.

Continuing south towards Lossiemouth an oil rig appeared on my track. The controller chirped up and told me I was too close and needed to climb immediately or make a 90 degree turn to the East. I started to do both.

Apparently he wasn't happy about my progress and sounded bloody abrupt about it. In return I lost my temper.

When I use the radio I rehearse what I'm about to say and say it calmly. Not too fast and not too slow. There's no accent. I want to get my message across without confusion.

I was on the home straight having flown over 5,000 miles and been so uncomfortably low my Garmin thought I'd landed a

Decision Height

dozen more times than I had. This chap was going to get a broadside.

Unfortunately for him he asked for my flight details, *'pass your message'*, style. He got every morsel of information three times faster than normal and I had visions of him struggling to get his head round everything I'd trumpeted out.

There was a long pause from his end. And then I believe he decided to call a truce. From that point on he was very civil, even friendly. I bloody hate bullies and a lack of sleep had completely killed my patience.

He latterly said goodbye and I carried on with my trip south. Twenty minutes later a text flashed up on my phone from the chaps saying Kirkbride was a little misty and they were diverting to Carlisle. For some reason that made my face crease into a broad smile.

Jon Hilton

Changing course I landed at Carlisle. Climbed out of India Zulu and felt seriously 'fooked'. Pardon the language.

Decision Height

The other two aircraft were there and four fellas came over to say hi. Deepak and Tom of London Airsports plus Dave Mellor and Mark Donnelly from Barton.

We all shook hands and I thanked them for flying up to say hi. And because my bladder was bursting I made my excuses and headed towards the toilet.

Washing my hands I looked into the loo mirror and began asking my reflection why I'd put myself through the whole ordeal.

Drifting back to reality I noticed that I'd acquired a cracking pair of man tits whilst I'd been away. The instant resolution was to avoid all confectionary products in the future.

The five of us had a cup of tea and twenty minutes later were saddling up. On this leg Dave came along with me.

There was a certain amount of mist along the way and for some reason I took the lead and the other aircraft flew to my left and right. I was speaking to various folk on the radio on behalf of our formation.

One comment to make, to blow my own trumpet, is that my mate Dave took a long look at me as we were sat side by side and said, *'I've got to say you sound quite professional on the radio'*.

Our friendship is based on mocking each other hence his words seemed out of place. Silly old sod. I frowned and gave him a good natured stare.

We made it to Barton, buzzed the tower, and lined up to land. Dave kept looking at the ASI as we slowed and started descending.

Jon Hilton

The Dynon was showing an airspeed of 26 knots. Theoretically too slow to be airborne. He asked what the hell I was doing and I shrugged and made a light hearted comment about the Airspeed Indicator not working properly. That confused him.

Then the airspeed readings disappeared all together and his silence suggested he wasn't enjoying himself.

We crossed the runway threshold with 2,000ft of grass to play with. I'd lost all feeling for the aircraft and been too fast, been way too long into the runway and floated too far.

Samson stopped rolling with maybe 100ft to spare.

We taxied onto the apron and I tumbled out of the aircraft and lay on the tarmac. I'd flown for nearly four hours and after 'everything' that was my absolute limit...

I couldn't have flown for another minute.

Steve Cooke & Dave Bremner of the BMAA appeared. Thoroughly nice chaps.

We all shared a bottle of Champagne to celebrate the fact I wasn't dead.

Decision Height

Then I walked over to the Tower and set about completing the Arrival book.

For a second I couldn't recall where I'd taken off from. The question asked "arrived from"... And being too tired to think I simply wrote down, Canada.

Seventeen days away. 2 days due to Greenland closing on Sundays. 3 days bureaucracy. 4 days of bad weather. 8 days flying.

The End.

PS. This last picture is of my beautiful little daughter who seemed happy to receive the presents I'd bought. I was stupid for taking on the trip and jeopardising her future.

Decision Height

There are a lot of legitimate and practical reasons why Microlights don't traverse oceans. I was very, very lucky and don't recommend the trip unless you have de-icing gear on the aircraft and an autopilot.

Plus a toilet, hostess and jet engines would be excellent additions to the list.

Chapter 23 - Postscript - Back to reality

I went back to work the following day. At lunchtime I was in the queue at the Co-op buying the 3 items for £3.00, meal deal. Very mundane. Incredibly so.

The decision being a Tuna Mayonnaise or a Chicken Salad sandwich to go with my orange drink and Crunchie.

No life or death issues and for some reason I felt out of place....

A friend of mine described the trip as my Everest and I guess it was. I think we should all visit the horizon from time to time as a way of experiencing life.

What have I learnt? Life is precious but some of us seem compelled to test ourselves and see new things to appreciate how lucky we are. For the rest, life goes on regardless.

I'd like to say the story ends here, but should add the following. This trip is dedicated to my Dad who died 2 days later.

Dad was the youngest son of a Coal Man. He became an accountant and stashed away a million throughout the course of his working life (although I never saw any of it, the tight bugger). With mum by his side they raised 3 kids along the way.

Rest in Peace Mr Geoffrey Francis Hilton.

Decision Height

Flights.

Barton - Wick. 4hrs

Wick - Faroes. 2hrs 35

Vagar - Akureyri. 3hrs 40

Akureyri - Kulusuk. 5hrs 35

Kulusuk - Narsass. 4hrs 55

Narsass - Nuuk. 3hrs

Nuuk - Iqaluit. 5hrs

Iqaluit - Nuuk. 5hrs 15

Nuuk - Narsass. 3hrs 50

Narsass - Kulusuk. 5hrs 55

Kulusuk - Rekjavik. 4hrs 40

Rekjavik - Vagar. 5hrs

Vagar - Wick. 2hrs 45

Wick - Carlisle. 2hrs 25

Carlisle - Barton. 1hrs 20

Note. The above figures are taken from the Garmin 795. My 496 suggested longer flight times. Both are a tad unreliable as each thought I'd put the wheels down more often than I had, hence they'd stopped recording flight times.

237

Jon Hilton

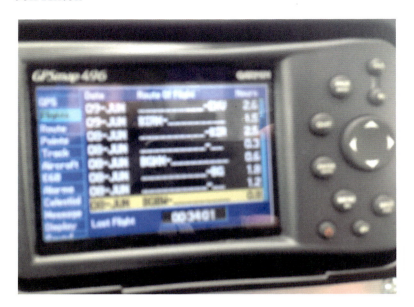

Chapter 24 - Jon Hilton, so far.

This rambles all over the place but I'm the person I am courtesy of the following...

I left school with 5 GCSE's. Picked up an ONC in Civil Engineering, fluked the Mensa tests (couldn't manage it now) and passed the Chartered Insurance Institute Financial Planning exams. I could once put the letters MLIA (dip) after my name.

Work wise I'm... a former Civil Engineering 'Estimator', Tunnel Engineer, Estate Agent (sorry), Mortgage Broker, Insurance Broker, Sales Manager for a House Building firm, Export Clerk, Project Manager for a lighting firm, Solicitors salesman and more recently a director of Legal Brokers Ltd.

My two claims to fame are being the project manager for the lighting on the "Wobbly Millennium Bridge" across the Thames. I secured the order and managed the installation.

Additionally I also did the demo's and secured the Searchlight orders for the Eiffel Tower. Two very smart projects to be involved with.

And I worked on the intank lighting for 'The Deep' which, at the time, was Europe's Deepest Water Aquarium. I was involved with the Kuwait PIFSS building and, in a clumsy way, helped design certain light fittings for both the Disney Cruise Ships and the Copenhagen Opera House.

Jon Hilton

Once upon a time I managed to blag my way into the Man United trophy room to fit a DMX light fitting.

Much more impressively I got a 25 yard swimming certificate at the age of 7. I've still got it.

Less impressively I managed the Bronze Duke of Edinburgh's award and the Berlin, Paris, New York, Moscow, Rekjavik and LA Marathons. The San Diego triathlon. A sponsored bike ride around Beijing (and did a luge type thing off the Great Wall), the Pamplona Bull Run and the Ironman.

Although I call it the Tinman because it's a damn silly name to call something....

On a couple of my trips I've had to sleep rough and don't advise sleeping on the streets of Berlin (during Autumn) or Paris or even Pamplona. Not pleasant experiences. You fear for your safety all the time, are cold, and generally feel hellishly tired.

Plus folk look down at you and sneer. Can't help themselves. Not a nice experience and one that changed my perspective on a few things. The moral of this paragraph? Buying a Big Issue occasionally is good for the soul.

I've managed a relay Swim across the Channel and, somehow, picked up a Blackbelt in JuJitzu. That period of my life generated three broken toes, broken finger, broken rib and foolishly a broken hand bone that needed surgery.

The latter was completely my fault. Essentially an argument with a wall. If it'd been plasterboard I'd have gone through it. Bricks are more robust, unfortunately. All very, very stupid on my part.

I've been to Canada, a dozen US States, Scandinavia, most of Europe, got chased by muggers in Kenya, went swimming off

Decision Height

Australia's Gold Coast and came within a whisker of being swept out to sea.

Went on a work trip to Dubai and briefly got taken into custody by the customs chaps. They suspected the 2 dozen promotional videos I'd taken, of searchlights, we're in fact pornographic. Within 60 seconds of watching the first video they got bored and released me.

We put a few Xenon searchlights on top of Sunderland's Stadium of Light hence I got invited to the VIP opening. I worked, a little, on the Millennium Dome and wandered around the James Bond set, at Pinewood Studios, whilst dropping off some kit.

I've climbed to the very top of Canary Wharf Tower. After you've navigated past all the air conditioning machinery there's an access hatch in the roof void and I poked my head out. At the time it was Europe's highest building.

As incidentals I've had the Glastonbury and Silverstone Grand Prix experiences. I don't smoke and I'm not a druggie but I did try Space cakes at Glastonbury and that was good fun. Silverstone? Bit of a dump. Couldn't hear anything above the sound of the cars and had no idea what the hell was happening

In general airborne terms, I've Bunjee jumped, held my basic Hang Gliding and Sky Diving licences.

I was 21 or 22 when I went to Missouri to get my PPL. During my stay the Chief Flying Instructor got arrested for suspected drug running and that extended my time over there by a couple of months.

Interestingly I was offered a job as a 'trainee' crop spraying pilot. Apart from having to pick up a Commercial rating, like you do, the 6 month induction process meant standing in various fields waiving a pair of paddles above my head.

241

Jon Hilton

The intent was that a more experienced pilot would then aim at me, swoop down from the skies, and drop chemicals on both myself and the nearby crops. Not an ideal way to spend your day if you're the poor so and so on the ground.

I sometimes regret not using the job as a platform to get a Green Card but latterly decided to give that opportunity a miss. I'm proud to be a Brit.

I've flown, on my little lonesome, into Daytona International (directly above the Speedway), as well as through the Bermuda Triangle to Freeport International in the Bahamas.

On the way back I was cleared by the military Controller to fly directly above the runway, at Cape Canaveral, where the Space Shuttle used to land. Midnight at that point, pitch black. Quite an intense experience.

On two occasions I've flown into Orlando International. Which was bloody intimidating in a Cessna 152. And during the same period witnessed two "night time" Space Shuttle launches which were bloody amazing. Awe inspiring. Check them out online if you're curious.

In overall terms I've held or passed the following; US PPL, UK PPL, IMC rating, Night rating, RT rating, Multi Engine and Microlight ratings.

Please note, having passed the IMC and Multi Engine flying and written exams I didn't have the funds to pay for the licences themselves hence these ratings fell by the wayside immediately.

It's a more complicated story, and it involved a lady who didn't want me to fly, but that was the final straw and I gave up on aviation for 10 or so years.

After starting to fly Microlights I took my CT to both the Alps and the Chitty Chitty Bang Bang Castle. And then fluked the GPS

Decision Height

category of the 2012 Round Britain Microlight rally, coming away with a trophy.

Completely the wrong place to add this but it's vaguely interesting. Two and a half decades ago, for 1 second, I held Michael Jackson's attention after being dragged to Aintree to watch him perform.

Half a dozen of us were a couple of rows back from the stage. Sunny day. According to Wikipedia, 125,000 people were there.

Everyone was chanting Billy Jean or some such. I'd got into the swing of things by then and was singing my lungs out. Unfortunately I got the lyrics completely wrong and was singing/shouting when everyone else damn well wasn't. Michael looked over. So did everyone around me. I felt like such a burke.

I've done the African safari trip and to my eternal shame the Marlin fishing 'thing' in the West Indies. We didn't catch anything big, the plan was to put it back if we had, but we did snag a little tiddler.

It's one of my great regrets that I didn't stand up to the boat crew and tell them to put the bugger back over the side. I should have had bigger balls. I won't go into more detail but that's been my 'silence of the lambs' moment ever since.... Bloody 'orrible it was.

Getting back to the boring stuff, I've had an Early Day Motion listed in the House of Commons which was supported by 7 MP's. It's a long story but in essence I have a distinct sense of right and wrong.

Ten or so years ago I set up Legal Brokers Ltd with a £300 over draft and our turnover peaked at £1million. Which sounds quite good but years ago realised I didn't like the person I was turning into and I've taken my foot of the pedal.

243

Jon Hilton

Money doesn't equal happiness, I'd suggest.

The funny thing is that whilst I've had an interesting time with various things, no matter what I do, I get bored. I've written all this, and it's as if none of it's happened.

Possibly I need something else to put my mind too.

Jon Hilton

www.justgiving.com/jon-hilton

Decision Height

Chapter 24 – One Year on.

When I originally looked at doing the trip I found a fella, via Google, who'd done a continent hopping trip in a Microlight.

I called and his wife answered. I explained what I was trying to do and she listened quietly, then said, "*please don't go, you'll probably die*".

I guess I can be pig headed sometimes and wasn't put off.

Immediately after returning from the trip, shaken and dazed, I wrote a draft of the experiences I'd been through. Then started reading bits, here and there, and wasn't happy with the grammar etc. I'm still not.

It's taken me a year or so to finish it off because I've subsequently realised the trip was more intimately linked to my dad dying than I'd thought.

At the time I guess I just wanted to 'fly away' and focus on anything other than one of the constants in my life fading from existence. And Canada ticked a few boxes.

Hence trying to tidy this up for publication has been a difficult experience and one I haven't enjoyed.

If it wasn't for the following I would have let the story die.

Upon my return another chap contacted me and wanted to replicate the flight. I tried my damndest to put him off but ultimately we swapped a couple of dozen emails regards my thoughts and suggestions.

Jon Hilton

Hence I've finally got my act together and finished this story as a salutary warning to other aviators about the perils of the North Atlantic.

It is not a trip to be taken lightly and I wouldn't recommend it in a VFR only aircraft. I know of two professional pilots who've died since I got back. One in Akureyri and one in Kulusuk.

Hence as a final comment if you're reading this and want an adventure might I respectfully suggest somewhere warm might be a better idea.

Otherwise someone will perish and I'd rather not have that on my conscience.

JH

Printed in Great Britain
by Amazon